Arbitration Act 1996

CHAPTER 23

Explanatory Notes are available separately

GRANGIS UK Publishing

Adapted and published by GRANGIS (Grand Register Library).
Online: www.grangis.com
E-mail: contact@grangis.com

In this version:
ISBN: 979-8-88559-005-1

Note: This is the original version (as it was originally enacted). Title, sub-title and the generated date is as marked on the pages.

Arbitration Act 1996

CHAPTER 23

ARBITRATION ACT 1996

PART I

ARBITRATION PURSUANT TO AN ARBITRATION AGREEMENT

Introductory

The arbitration agreement

Stay of legal proceedings

Commencement of arbitral proceedings

The arbitral tribunal

Jurisdiction of the arbitral tribunal

The arbitral proceedings

Powers of court in relation to arbitral proceedings

The award

Costs of the arbitration

Powers of the court in relation to award

Miscellaneous

Supplementary

PART II

OTHER PROVISIONS RELATING TO ARBITRATION

Domestic arbitration agreements

Consumer arbitration agreements

General

2 (1) Subject to the following provisions of this Schedule, references...

Arbitrator's fees

3 (1) The power of the court in section 28(2) to...

Exercise of court powers in support of arbitration

4 (1) Where the arbitral tribunal consists of or includes a...

Extension of time for making award

5 (1) The power conferred by section 50 (extension of time...

Withholding award in case of non-payment

6 (1) The provisions of paragraph 7 apply in place of...
7 (1) A judge-arbitrator may refuse to deliver an award except...

Correction of award or additional award

8 Subsections (4) to (6) of section 57 (correction of award...

Costs

9 Where the arbitral tribunal consists of or includes a judge-arbitrator...
10 (1) The power of the court under section 64 to...

Enforcement of award

11 The leave of the court required by section 66 (enforcement...

Solicitors' costs

12 The powers of the court to make declarations and orders...

Powers of court in relation to service of documents

13 (1) The power of the court under section 77(2) (powers...

Powers of court to extend time limits relating to arbitral proceedings

14 (1) The power conferred by section 79 (power of court...

SCHEDULE 3 — Consequential amendments

Merchant Shipping Act 1894 (c. 60)

1 In section 496 of the Merchant Shipping Act 1894 (provisions...

Stannaries Court (Abolition) Act 1896 (c. 45)

2 In section 4(1) of the Stannaries Court (Abolition) Act 1896...

Tithe Act 1936 (c. 43)

3 In section 39(1) of the Tithe Act 1936 (proceedings of...

Education Act 1944 (c. 31)

4 In section 75(2) of the Education Act 1944 (proceedings of...

Commonwealth Telegraphs Act 1949 (c. 39)

5 In section 8(2) of the Commonwealth Telegraphs Act 1949 (proceedings...

Lands Tribunal Act 1949 (c. 42)

6 In section 3 of the Lands Tribunal Act 1949 (proceedings...

Wireless Telegraphy Act 1949 (c. 54)

7 In the Wireless Telegraphy Act 1949, Schedule 2 (procedure of...

Patents Act 1949 (c. 87)

8 In section 67 of the Patents Act 1949 (proceedings as...

National Health Service (Amendment) Act 1949 (c. 93)

9 In section 7(8) of the National Health Service (Amendment) Act...

Arbitration Act 1950 (c. 27)

10 In section 36(1) of the Arbitration Act 1950 (effect of...

Interpretation Act (Northern Ireland) 1954 (c. 33 (N.I.))

11 In section 46(2) of the Interpretation Act (Northern Ireland) 1954...

Agricultural Marketing Act 1958 (c. 47)

12 In section 12(1) of the Agricultural Marketing Act 1958 (application...

Carriage by Air Act 1961 (c. 27)

13 (1) The Carriage by Air Act 1961 is amended as...

Factories Act 1961 (c. 34)

14 In the Factories Act 1961, for section 171 (application of...

Clergy Pensions Measure 1961 (No. 3)

15 In the Clergy Pensions Measure 1961, section 38(4) (determination of...

Transport Act 1962 (c. 46)

16 (1) The Transport Act 1962 is amended as follows.

Corn Rents Act 1963 (c. 14)

17 In the Corn Rents Act 1963, section 1(5) (schemes for...

Plant Varieties and Seeds Act 1964 (c. 14)

18 In section 10(6) of the Plant Varieties and Seeds Act...

Lands Tribunal and Compensation Act (Northern Ireland) 1964 (c. 29 (N.I.))

19 In section 9 of the Lands Tribunal and Compensation Act...

Industrial and Provident Societies Act 1965 (c. 12)

20 (1) Section 60 of the Industrial and Provident Societies Act...

Carriage of Goods by Road Act 1965 (c. 37)

21 In section 7(2) of the Carriage of Goods by Road...

Factories Act (Northern Ireland) 1965 (c. 20 (N.I.))

22 In section 171 of the Factories Act (Northern Ireland) 1965...

Commonwealth Secretariat Act 1966 (c. 10)

23 In section 1(3) of the Commonwealth Secretariat Act 1966 (contracts...

Arbitration (International Investment Disputes) Act 1966 (c. 41)

24 In the Arbitration (International Investment Disputes) Act 1966, for section...

Poultry Improvement Act (Northern Ireland) 1968 (c. 12 (N.I.))

25 In paragraph 10(4) of the Schedule to the Poultry Improvement...

Industrial and Provident Societies Act (Northern Ireland) 1969 (c. 24 (N.I.))

26 (1) Section 69 of the Industrial and Provident Societies Act...

Health and Personal Social Services (Northern Ireland) Order 1972 (N.I.14)

27 In Article 105(6) of the Health and Personal Social Services...

Consumer Credit Act 1974 (c. 39)

28 (1) Section 146 of the Consumer Credit Act 1974 is...

Friendly Societies Act 1974 (c. 46)

29 (1) The Friendly Societies Act 1974 is amended as follows....

Industry Act 1975 (c. 68)

30 In Schedule 3 to the Industry Act (arbitration of disputes...

Industrial Relations (Northern Ireland) Order 1976 (N.I.16)

31 In Article 59(9) of the Industrial Relations (Northern Ireland) Order...

Aircraft and Shipbuilding Industries Act 1977 (c. 3)

32 In Schedule 7 to the Aircraft and Shipbuilding Industries Act...

Patents Act 1977 (c. 37)

33 In section 130 of the Patents Act 1977 (interpretation), in...

Judicature (Northern Ireland) Act 1978 (c. 23)

34 (1) The Judicature (Northern Ireland) Act 1978 is amended as...

Health and Safety at Work (Northern Ireland) Order 1978 (N.I.9)

35 In Schedule 4 to the Health and Safety at Work...

County Courts (Northern Ireland) Order 1980 (N.I.3)

36 (1) The County Courts (Northern Ireland) Order 1980 is amended...

Supreme Court Act 1981 (c. 54)

37 (1) The Supreme Court Act 1981 is amended as follows....

Merchant Shipping (Liner Conferences) Act 1982 (c. 37)

38 In section 7(5) of the Merchant Shipping (Liner Conferences) Act...

Agricultural Marketing (Northern Ireland) Order 1982 (N.I.12)

39 In Article 14 of the Agricultural Marketing (Northern Ireland) Order...

Mental Health Act 1983 (c. 20)

40 In section 78 of the Mental Health Act 1983 (procedure...

Registered Homes Act 1984 (c. 23)

41 In section 43 of the Registered Homes Act 1984 (procedure...

Housing Act 1985 (c. 68)

42 In section 47(3) of the Housing Act 1985 (agreement as...

Landlord and Tenant Act 1985 (c. 70)

43 In section 19(3) of the Landlord and Tenant Act 1985...

Credit Unions (Northern Ireland) Order 1985 (N.I.12)

44 (1) Article 72 of the Credit Unions (Northern Ireland) Order...

Agricultural Holdings Act 1986 (c. 5)

45 In section 84(1) of the Agricultural Holdings Act 1986 (provisions...

Insolvency Act 1986 (c. 45)

46 In the Insolvency Act 1986, after section 349 insert— Arbitration...

Building Societies Act 1986 (c. 53)

47 In Part II of Schedule 14 to the Building Societies...

Mental Health (Northern Ireland) Order 1986 (N.I.4)

48 In Article 83 of the Mental Health (Northern Ireland) Order...

Arbitration Act 1996

1996 CHAPTER 23

An Act to restate and improve the law relating to arbitration pursuant to an arbitration agreement; to make other provision relating to arbitration and arbitration awards; and for connected purposes. [17th June 1996]

Be it enacted by the Queen's most Excellent Majesty, by and with the advice and consent of the Lords Spiritual and Temporal, and Commons, in this present Parliament assembled, and by the authority of the same, as follows:—

PART I

ARBITRATION PURSUANT TO AN ARBITRATION AGREEMENT

Introductory

1 General principles

The provisions of this Part are founded on the following principles, and shall be construed accordingly—

(a) the object of arbitration is to obtain the fair resolution of disputes by an impartial tribunal without unnecessary delay or expense;

(b) the parties should be free to agree how their disputes are resolved, subject only to such safeguards as are necessary in the public interest;

(c) in matters governed by this Part the court should not intervene except as provided by this Part.

2 Scope of application of provisions

(1) The provisions of this Part apply where the seat of the arbitration is in England and Wales or Northern Ireland.

(2) The following sections apply even if the seat of the arbitration is outside England and Wales or Northern Ireland or no seat has been designated or determined—

(a) sections 9 to 11 (stay of legal proceedings, &c.), and

(b) section 66 (enforcement of arbitral awards).

(3) The powers conferred by the following sections apply even if the seat of the arbitration is outside England and Wales or Northern Ireland or no seat has been designated or determined—

(a) section 43 (securing the attendance of witnesses), and

(b) section 44 (court powers exercisable in support of arbitral proceedings);

but the court may refuse to exercise any such power if, in the opinion of the court, the fact that the seat of the arbitration is outside England and Wales or Northern Ireland, or that when designated or determined the seat is likely to be outside England and Wales or Northern Ireland, makes it inappropriate to do so.

(4) The court may exercise a power conferred by any provision of this Part not mentioned in subsection (2) or (3) for the purpose of supporting the arbitral process where—

(a) no seat of the arbitration has been designated or determined, and

(b) by reason of a connection with England and Wales or Northern Ireland the court is satisfied that it is appropriate to do so.

(5) Section 7 (separability of arbitration agreement) and section 8 (death of a party) apply where the law applicable to the arbitration agreement is the law of England and Wales or Northern Ireland even if the seat of the arbitration is outside England and Wales or Northern Ireland or has not been designated or determined.

3 The seat of the arbitration

In this Part "the seat of the arbitration" means the juridical seat of the arbitration designated—

(a) by the parties to the arbitration agreement, or

(b) by any arbitral or other institution or person vested by the parties with powers in that regard, or

(c) by the arbitral tribunal if so authorised by the parties,

or determined, in the absence of any such designation, having regard to the parties' agreement and all the relevant circumstances.

4 Mandatory and non-mandatory provisions

(1) The mandatory provisions of this Part are listed in Schedule 1 and have effect notwithstanding any agreement to the contrary.

(2) The other provisions of this Part (the "non-mandatory provisions") allow the parties to make their own arrangements by agreement but provide rules which apply in the absence of such agreement.

(3) The parties may make such arrangements by agreeing to the application of institutional rules or providing any other means by which a matter may be decided.

(4) It is immaterial whether or not the law applicable to the parties' agreement is the law of England and Wales or, as the case may be, Northern Ireland.

(5) The choice of a law other than the law of England and Wales or Northern Ireland as the applicable law in respect of a matter provided for by a non-mandatory provision of this Part is equivalent to an agreement making provision about that matter.

For this purpose an applicable law determined in accordance with the parties' agreement, or which is objectively determined in the absence of any express or implied choice, shall be treated as chosen by the parties.

5 Agreements to be in writing

(1) The provisions of this Part apply only where the arbitration agreement is in writing, and any other agreement between the parties as to any matter is effective for the purposes of this Part only if in writing.

The expressions "agreement", "agree" and "agreed" shall be construed accordingly.

(2) There is an agreement in writing—

(a) if the agreement is made in writing (whether or not it is signed by the parties),

(b) if the agreement is made by exchange of communications in writing, or

(c) if the agreement is evidenced in writing.

(3) Where parties agree otherwise than in writing by reference to terms which are in writing, they make an agreement in writing.

(4) An agreement is evidenced in writing if an agreement made otherwise than in writing is recorded by one of the parties, or by a third party, with the authority of the parties to the agreement.

(5) An exchange of written submissions in arbitral or legal proceedings in which the existence of an agreement otherwise than in writing is alleged by one party against another party and not denied by the other party in his response constitutes as between those parties an agreement in writing to the effect alleged.

(6) References in this Part to anything being written or in writing include its being recorded by any means.

The arbitration agreement

6 Definition of arbitration agreement

(1) In this Part an "arbitration agreement" means an agreement to submit to arbitration present or future disputes (whether they are contractual or not).

(2) The reference in an agreement to a written form of arbitration clause or to a document containing an arbitration clause constitutes an arbitration agreement if the reference is such as to make that clause part of the agreement.

7 Separability of arbitration agreement

Unless otherwise agreed by the parties, an arbitration agreement which forms or was intended to form part of another agreement (whether or not in writing) shall not be regarded as invalid, non-existent or ineffective because that other agreement is invalid, or did not come into existence or has become ineffective, and it shall for that purpose be treated as a distinct agreement.

8 Whether agreement discharged by death of a party

(1) Unless otherwise agreed by the parties, an arbitration agreement is not discharged by the death of a party and may be enforced by or against the personal representatives of that party.

(2) Subsection (1) does not affect the operation of any enactment or rule of law by virtue of which a substantive right or obligation is extinguished by death.

Stay of legal proceedings

9 Stay of legal proceedings

(1) A party to an arbitration agreement against whom legal proceedings are brought (whether by way of claim or counterclaim) in respect of a matter which under the agreement is to be referred to arbitration may (upon notice to the other parties to the proceedings) apply to the court in which the proceedings have been brought to stay the proceedings so far as they concern that matter.

(2) An application may be made notwithstanding that the matter is to be referred to arbitration only after the exhaustion of other dispute resolution procedures.

(3) An application may not be made by a person before taking the appropriate procedural step (if any) to acknowledge the legal proceedings against him or after he has taken any step in those proceedings to answer the substantive claim.

(4) On an application under this section the court shall grant a stay unless satisfied that the arbitration agreement is null and void, inoperative, or incapable of being performed.

(5) If the court refuses to stay the legal proceedings, any provision that an award is a condition precedent to the bringing of legal proceedings in respect of any matter is of no effect in relation to those proceedings.

10 Reference of interpleader issue to arbitration

(1) Where in legal proceedings relief by way of interpleader is granted and any issue between the claimants is one in respect of which there is an arbitration agreement between them, the court granting the relief shall direct that the issue be determined in accordance with the agreement unless the circumstances are such that proceedings brought by a claimant in respect of the matter would not be stayed.

(2) Where subsection (1) applies but the court does not direct that the issue be determined in accordance with the arbitration agreement, any provision that an award is a condition precedent to the bringing of legal proceedings in respect of any matter shall not affect the determination of that issue by the court.

11 Retention of security where Admiralty proceedings stayed

(1) Where Admiralty proceedings are stayed on the ground that the dispute in question should be submitted to arbitration, the court granting the stay may, if in those

proceedings property has been arrested or bail or other security has been given to prevent or obtain release from arrest—

(a) order that the property arrested be retained as security for the satisfaction of any award given in the arbitration in respect of that dispute, or

(b) order that the stay of those proceedings be conditional on the provision of equivalent security for the satisfaction of any such award.

(2) Subject to any provision made by rules of court and to any necessary modifications, the same law and practice shall apply in relation to property retained in pursuance of an order as would apply if it were held for the purposes of proceedings in the court making the order.

Commencement of arbitral proceedings

12 Power of court to extend time for beginning arbitral proceedings, &c

(1) Where an arbitration agreement to refer future disputes to arbitration provides that a claim shall be barred, or the claimant's right extinguished, unless the claimant takes within a time fixed by the agreement some step—

(a) to begin arbitral proceedings, or

(b) to begin other dispute resolution procedures which must be exhausted before arbitral proceedings can be begun,

the court may by order extend the time for taking that step.

(2) Any party to the arbitration agreement may apply for such an order (upon notice to the other parties), but only after a claim has arisen and after exhausting any available arbitral process for obtaining an extension of time.

(3) The court shall make an order only if satisfied—

(a) that the circumstances are such as were outside the reasonable contemplation of the parties when they agreed the provision in question, and that it would be just to extend the time, or

(b) that the conduct of one party makes it unjust to hold the other party to the strict terms of the provision in question.

(4) The court may extend the time for such period and on such terms as it thinks fit, and may do so whether or not the time previously fixed (by agreement or by a previous order) has expired.

(5) An order under this section does not affect the operation of the Limitation Acts (see section 13).

(6) The leave of the court is required for any appeal from a decision of the court under this section.

13 Application of Limitation Acts

(1) The Limitation Acts apply to arbitral proceedings as they apply to legal proceedings.

(2) The court may order that in computing the time prescribed by the Limitation Acts for the commencement of proceedings (including arbitral proceedings) in respect of a dispute which was the subject matter—

(a) of an award which the court orders to be set aside or declares to be of no effect, or

(b) of the affected part of an award which the court orders to be set aside in part, or declares to be in part of no effect,

the period between the commencement of the arbitration and the date of the order referred to in paragraph (a) or (b) shall be excluded.

(3) In determining for the purposes of the Limitation Acts when a cause of action accrued, any provision that an award is a condition precedent to the bringing of legal proceedings in respect of a matter to which an arbitration agreement applies shall be disregarded.

(4) In this Part "the Limitation Acts" means—

(a) in England and Wales, the Limitation Act 1980, the Foreign Limitation Periods Act 1984 and any other enactment (whenever passed) relating to the limitation of actions;

(b) in Northern Ireland, the Limitation (Northern Ireland) Order 1989, the Foreign Limitation Periods (Northern Ireland) Order 1985 and any other enactment (whenever passed) relating to the limitation of actions.

14 Commencement of arbitral proceedings

(1) The parties are free to agree when arbitral proceedings are to be regarded as commenced for the purposes of this Part and for the purposes of the Limitation Acts.

(2) If there is no such agreement the following provisions apply.

(3) Where the arbitrator is named or designated in the arbitration agreement, arbitral proceedings are commenced in respect of a matter when one party serves on the other party or parties a notice in writing requiring him or them to submit that matter to the person so named or designated.

(4) Where the arbitrator or arbitrators are to be appointed by the parties, arbitral proceedings are commenced in respect of a matter when one party serves on the other party or parties notice in writing requiring him or them to appoint an arbitrator or to agree to the appointment of an arbitrator in respect of that matter.

(5) Where the arbitrator or arbitrators are to be appointed by a person other than a party to the proceedings, arbitral proceedings are commenced in respect of a matter when one party gives notice in writing to that person requesting him to make the appointment in respect of that matter.

The arbitral tribunal

15 The arbitral tribunal

(1) The parties are free to agree on the number of arbitrators to form the tribunal and whether there is to be a chairman or umpire.

(2) Unless otherwise agreed by the parties, an agreement that the number of arbitrators shall be two or any other even number shall be understood as requiring the appointment of an additional arbitrator as chairman of the tribunal.

(3) If there is no agreement as to the number of arbitrators, the tribunal shall consist of a sole arbitrator.

16 Procedure for appointment of arbitrators

(1) The parties are free to agree on the procedure for appointing the arbitrator or arbitrators, including the procedure for appointing any chairman or umpire.

(2) If or to the extent that there is no such agreement, the following provisions apply.

(3) If the tribunal is to consist of a sole arbitrator, the parties shall jointly appoint the arbitrator not later than 28 days after service of a request in writing by either party to do so.

(4) If the tribunal is to consist of two arbitrators, each party shall appoint one arbitrator not later than 14 days after service of a request in writing by either party to do so.

(5) If the tribunal is to consist of three arbitrators—

(a) each party shall appoint one arbitrator not later than 14 days after service of a request in writing by either party to do so, and

(b) the two so appointed shall forthwith appoint a third arbitrator as the chairman of the tribunal.

(6) If the tribunal is to consist of two arbitrators and an umpire—

(a) each party shall appoint one arbitrator not later than 14 days after service of a request in writing by either party to do so, and

(b) the two so appointed may appoint an umpire at any time after they themselves are appointed and shall do so before any substantive hearing or forthwith if they cannot agree on a matter relating to the arbitration.

(7) In any other case (in particular, if there are more than two parties) section 18 applies as in the case of a failure of the agreed appointment procedure.

17 Power in case of default to appoint sole arbitrator

(1) Unless the parties otherwise agree, where each of two parties to an arbitration agreement is to appoint an arbitrator and one party ("the party in default") refuses to do so, or fails to do so within the time specified, the other party, having duly appointed his arbitrator, may give notice in writing to the party in default that he proposes to appoint his arbitrator to act as sole arbitrator.

(2) If the party in default does not within 7 clear days of that notice being given—

(a) make the required appointment, and

(b) notify the other party that he has done so,

the other party may appoint his arbitrator as sole arbitrator whose award shall be binding on both parties as if he had been so appointed by agreement.

(3) Where a sole arbitrator has been appointed under subsection (2), the party in default may (upon notice to the appointing party) apply to the court which may set aside the appointment.

(4) The leave of the court is required for any appeal from a decision of the court under this section.

18 Failure of appointment procedure

(1) The parties are free to agree what is to happen in the event of a failure of the procedure for the appointment of the arbitral tribunal.

There is no failure if an appointment is duly made under section 17 (power in case of default to appoint sole arbitrator), unless that appointment is set aside.

(2) If or to the extent that there is no such agreement any party to the arbitration agreement may (upon notice to the other parties) apply to the court to exercise its powers under this section.

(3) Those powers are—

(a) to give directions as to the making of any necessary appointments;

(b) to direct that the tribunal shall be constituted by such appointments (or any one or more of them) as have been made;

(c) to revoke any appointments already made;

(d) to make any necessary appointments itself.

(4) An appointment made by the court under this section has effect as if made with the agreement of the parties.

(5) The leave of the court is required for any appeal from a decision of the court under this section.

19 Court to have regard to agreed qualifications

In deciding whether to exercise, and in considering how to exercise, any of its powers under section 16 (procedure for appointment of arbitrators) or section 18 (failure of appointment procedure), the court shall have due regard to any agreement of the parties as to the qualifications required of the arbitrators.

20 Chairman

(1) Where the parties have agreed that there is to be a chairman, they are free to agree what the functions of the chairman are to be in relation to the making of decisions, orders and awards.

(2) If or to the extent that there is no such agreement, the following provisions apply.

(3) Decisions, orders and awards shall be made by all or a majority of the arbitrators (including the chairman).

(4) The view of the chairman shall prevail in relation to a decision, order or award in respect of which there is neither unanimity nor a majority under subsection (3).

21 Umpire

(1) Where the parties have agreed that there is to be an umpire, they are free to agree what the functions of the umpire are to be, and in particular—

(a) whether he is to attend the proceedings, and

(b) when he is to replace the other arbitrators as the tribunal with power to make decisions, orders and awards.

(2) If or to the extent that there is no such agreement, the following provisions apply.

(3) The umpire shall attend the proceedings and be supplied with the same documents and other materials as are supplied to the other arbitrators.

(4) Decisions, orders and awards shall be made by the other arbitrators unless and until they cannot agree on a matter relating to the arbitration.

In that event they shall forthwith give notice in writing to the parties and the umpire, whereupon the umpire shall replace them as the tribunal with power to make decisions, orders and awards as if he were sole arbitrator.

(5) If the arbitrators cannot agree but fail to give notice of that fact, or if any of them fails to join in the giving of notice, any party to the arbitral proceedings may (upon notice to the other parties and to the tribunal) apply to the court which may order that the umpire shall replace the other arbitrators as the tribunal with power to make decisions, orders and awards as if he were sole arbitrator.

(6) The leave of the court is required for any appeal from a decision of the court under this section.

22 Decision-making where no chairman or umpire

(1) Where the parties agree that there shall be two or more arbitrators with no chairman or umpire, the parties are free to agree how the tribunal is to make decisions, orders and awards.

(2) If there is no such agreement, decisions, orders and awards shall be made by all or a majority of the arbitrators.

23 Revocation of arbitrator's authority

(1) The parties are free to agree in what circumstances the authority of an arbitrator may be revoked.

(2) If or to the extent that there is no such agreement the following provisions apply.

(3) The authority of an arbitrator may not be revoked except—

- (a) by the parties acting jointly, or
- (b) by an arbitral or other institution or person vested by the parties with powers in that regard.

(4) Revocation of the authority of an arbitrator by the parties acting jointly must be agreed in writing unless the parties also agree (whether or not in writing) to terminate the arbitration agreement.

(5) Nothing in this section affects the power of the court—

- (a) to revoke an appointment under section 18 (powers exercisable in case of failure of appointment procedure), or
- (b) to remove an arbitrator on the grounds specified in section 24.

24 Power of court to remove arbitrator

(1) A party to arbitral proceedings may (upon notice to the other parties, to the arbitrator concerned and to any other arbitrator) apply to the court to remove an arbitrator on any of the following grounds—

(a) that circumstances exist that give rise to justifiable doubts as to his impartiality;

(b) that he does not possess the qualifications required by the arbitration agreement;

(c) that he is physically or mentally incapable of conducting the proceedings or there are justifiable doubts as to his capacity to do so;

(d) that he has refused or failed—

(i) properly to conduct the proceedings, or

(ii) to use all reasonable despatch in conducting the proceedings or making an award,

and that substantial injustice has been or will be caused to the applicant.

(2) If there is an arbitral or other institution or person vested by the parties with power to remove an arbitrator, the court shall not exercise its power of removal unless satisfied that the applicant has first exhausted any available recourse to that institution or person.

(3) The arbitral tribunal may continue the arbitral proceedings and make an award while an application to the court under this section is pending.

(4) Where the court removes an arbitrator, it may make such order as it thinks fit with respect to his entitlement (if any) to fees or expenses, or the repayment of any fees or expenses already paid.

(5) The arbitrator concerned is entitled to appear and be heard by the court before it makes any order under this section.

(6) The leave of the court is required for any appeal from a decision of the court under this section.

25 Resignation of arbitrator

(1) The parties are free to agree with an arbitrator as to the consequences of his resignation as regards—

(a) his entitlement (if any) to fees or expenses, and

(b) any liability thereby incurred by him.

(2) If or to the extent that there is no such agreement the following provisions apply.

(3) An arbitrator who resigns his appointment may (upon notice to the parties) apply to the court—

(a) to grant him relief from any liability thereby incurred by him, and

(b) to make such order as it thinks fit with respect to his entitlement (if any) to fees or expenses or the repayment of any fees or expenses already paid.

(4) If the court is satisfied that in all the circumstances it was reasonable for the arbitrator to resign, it may grant such relief as is mentioned in subsection (3)(a) on such terms as it thinks fit.

(5) The leave of the court is required for any appeal from a decision of the court under this section.

26 Death of arbitrator or person appointing him

(1) The authority of an arbitrator is personal and ceases on his death.

(2) Unless otherwise agreed by the parties, the death of the person by whom an arbitrator was appointed does not revoke the arbitrator's authority.

27 Filling of vacancy, &c

(1) Where an arbitrator ceases to hold office, the parties are free to agree—

(a) whether and if so how the vacancy is to be filled,

(b) whether and if so to what extent the previous proceedings should stand, and

(c) what effect (if any) his ceasing to hold office has on any appointment made by him (alone or jointly).

(2) If or to the extent that there is no such agreement, the following provisions apply.

(3) The provisions of sections 16 (procedure for appointment of arbitrators) and 18 (failure of appointment procedure) apply in relation to the filling of the vacancy as in relation to an original appointment.

(4) The tribunal (when reconstituted) shall determine whether and if so to what extent the previous proceedings should stand.

This does not affect any right of a party to challenge those proceedings on any ground which had arisen before the arbitrator ceased to hold office.

(5) His ceasing to hold office does not affect any appointment by him (alone or jointly) of another arbitrator, in particular any appointment of a chairman or umpire.

28 Joint and several liability of parties to arbitrators for fees and expenses

(1) The parties are jointly and severally liable to pay to the arbitrators such reasonable fees and expenses (if any) as are appropriate in the circumstances.

(2) Any party may apply to the court (upon notice to the other parties and to the arbitrators) which may order that the amount of the arbitrators' fees and expenses shall be considered and adjusted by such means and upon such terms as it may direct.

(3) If the application is made after any amount has been paid to the arbitrators by way of fees or expenses, the court may order the repayment of such amount (if any) as is shown to be excessive, but shall not do so unless it is shown that it is reasonable in the circumstances to order repayment.

(4) The above provisions have effect subject to any order of the court under section 24(4) or 25(3)(b) (order as to entitlement to fees or expenses in case of removal or resignation of arbitrator).

(5) Nothing in this section affects any liability of a party to any other party to pay all or any of the costs of the arbitration (see sections 59 to 65) or any contractual right of an arbitrator to payment of his fees and expenses.

(6) In this section references to arbitrators include an arbitrator who has ceased to act and an umpire who has not replaced the other arbitrators.

29 Immunity of arbitrator

(1) An arbitrator is not liable for anything done or omitted in the discharge or purported discharge of his functions as arbitrator unless the act or omission is shown to have been in bad faith.

(2) Subsection (1) applies to an employee or agent of an arbitrator as it applies to the arbitrator himself.

(3) This section does not affect any liability incurred by an arbitrator by reason of his resigning (but see section 25).

Jurisdiction of the arbitral tribunal

30 Competence of tribunal to rule on its own jurisdiction

(1) Unless otherwise agreed by the parties, the arbitral tribunal may rule on its own substantive jurisdiction, that is, as to—

(a) whether there is a valid arbitration agreement,

(b) whether the tribunal is properly constituted, and

(c) what matters have been submitted to arbitration in accordance with the arbitration agreement.

(2) Any such ruling may be challenged by any available arbitral process of appeal or review or in accordance with the provisions of this Part.

31 Objection to substantive jurisdiction of tribunal

(1) An objection that the arbitral tribunal lacks substantive jurisdiction at the outset of the proceedings must be raised by a party not later than the time he takes the first step in the proceedings to contest the merits of any matter in relation to which he challenges the tribunal's jurisdiction.

A party is not precluded from raising such an objection by the fact that he has appointed or participated in the appointment of an arbitrator.

(2) Any objection during the course of the arbitral proceedings that the arbitral tribunal is exceeding its substantive jurisdiction must be made as soon as possible after the matter alleged to be beyond its jurisdiction is raised.

(3) The arbitral tribunal may admit an objection later than the time specified in subsection (1) or (2) if it considers the delay justified.

(4) Where an objection is duly taken to the tribunal's substantive jurisdiction and the tribunal has power to rule on its own jurisdiction, it may—

(a) rule on the matter in an award as to jurisdiction, or

(b) deal with the objection in its award on the merits.

If the parties agree which of these courses the tribunal should take, the tribunal shall proceed accordingly.

(5) The tribunal may in any case, and shall if the parties so agree, stay proceedings whilst an application is made to the court under section 32 (determination of preliminary point of jurisdiction).

32 Determination of preliminary point of jurisdiction

(1) The court may, on the application of a party to arbitral proceedings (upon notice to the other parties), determine any question as to the substantive jurisdiction of the tribunal.

A party may lose the right to object (see section 73).

(2) An application under this section shall not be considered unless—

(a) it is made with the agreement in writing of all the other parties to the proceedings, or

(b) it is made with the permission of the tribunal and the court is satisfied—

(i) that the determination of the question is likely to produce substantial savings in costs,

(ii) that the application was made without delay, and

(iii) that there is good reason why the matter should be decided by the court.

(3) An application under this section, unless made with the agreement of all the other parties to the proceedings, shall state the grounds on which it is said that the matter should be decided by the court.

(4) Unless otherwise agreed by the parties, the arbitral tribunal may continue the arbitral proceedings and make an award while an application to the court under this section is pending.

(5) Unless the court gives leave, no appeal lies from a decision of the court whether the conditions specified in subsection (2) are met.

(6) The decision of the court on the question of jurisdiction shall be treated as a judgment of the court for the purposes of an appeal.

But no appeal lies without the leave of the court which shall not be given unless the court considers that the question involves a point of law which is one of general importance or is one which for some other special reason should be considered by the Court of Appeal.

The arbitral proceedings

33 General duty of the tribunal

(1) The tribunal shall—

(a) act fairly and impartially as between the parties, giving each party a reasonable opportunity of putting his case and dealing with that of his opponent, and

(b) adopt procedures suitable to the circumstances of the particular case, avoiding unnecessary delay or expense, so as to provide a fair means for the resolution of the matters falling to be determined.

(2) The tribunal shall comply with that general duty in conducting the arbitral proceedings, in its decisions on matters of procedure and evidence and in the exercise of all other powers conferred on it.

34 Procedural and evidential matters

(1) It shall be for the tribunal to decide all procedural and evidential matters, subject to the right of the parties to agree any matter.

(2) Procedural and evidential matters include—

(a) when and where any part of the proceedings is to be held;

(b) the language or languages to be used in the proceedings and whether translations of any relevant documents are to be supplied;

(c) whether any and if so what form of written statements of claim and defence are to be used, when these should be supplied and the extent to which such statements can be later amended;

(d) whether any and if so which documents or classes of documents should be disclosed between and produced by the parties and at what stage;

(e) whether any and if so what questions should be put to and answered by the respective parties and when and in what form this should be done;

(f) whether to apply strict rules of evidence (or any other rules) as to the admissibility, relevance or weight of any material (oral, written or other) sought to be tendered on any matters of fact or opinion, and the time, manner and form in which such material should be exchanged and presented;

(g) whether and to what extent the tribunal should itself take the initiative in ascertaining the facts and the law;

(h) whether and to what extent there should be oral or written evidence or submissions.

(3) The tribunal may fix the time within which any directions given by it are to be complied with, and may if it thinks fit extend the time so fixed (whether or not it has expired).

35 Consolidation of proceedings and concurrent hearings

(1) The parties are free to agree—

(a) that the arbitral proceedings shall be consolidated with other arbitral proceedings, or

(b) that concurrent hearings shall be held,

on such terms as may be agreed.

(2) Unless the parties agree to confer such power on the tribunal, the tribunal has no power to order consolidation of proceedings or concurrent hearings.

36 Legal or other representation

Unless otherwise agreed by the parties, a party to arbitral proceedings may be represented in the proceedings by a lawyer or other person chosen by him.

37 Power to appoint experts, legal advisers or assessors

(1) Unless otherwise agreed by the parties—

(a) the tribunal may—

(i) appoint experts or legal advisers to report to it and the parties, or

(ii) appoint assessors to assist it on technical matters,

and may allow any such expert, legal adviser or assessor to attend the proceedings; and

(b) the parties shall be given a reasonable opportunity to comment on any information, opinion or advice offered by any such person.

(2) The fees and expenses of an expert, legal adviser or assessor appointed by the tribunal for which the arbitrators are liable are expenses of the arbitrators for the purposes of this Part.

38 General powers exercisable by the tribunal

(1) The parties are free to agree on the powers exercisable by the arbitral tribunal for the purposes of and in relation to the proceedings.

(2) Unless otherwise agreed by the parties the tribunal has the following powers.

(3) The tribunal may order a claimant to provide security for the costs of the arbitration.

This power shall not be exercised on the ground that the claimant is—

(a) an individual ordinarily resident outside the United Kingdom, or

(b) a corporation or association incorporated or formed under the law of a country outside the United Kingdom, or whose central management and control is exercised outside the United Kingdom.

(4) The tribunal may give directions in relation to any property which is the subject of the proceedings or as to which any question arises in the proceedings, and which is owned by or is in the possession of a party to the proceedings—

(a) for the inspection, photographing, preservation, custody or detention of the property by the tribunal, an expert or a party, or

(b) ordering that samples be taken from, or any observation be made of or experiment conducted upon, the property.

(5) The tribunal may direct that a party or witness shall be examined on oath or affirmation, and may for that purpose administer any necessary oath or take any necessary affirmation.

(6) The tribunal may give directions to a party for the preservation for the purposes of the proceedings of any evidence in his custody or control.

39 Power to make provisional awards

(1) The parties are free to agree that the tribunal shall have power to order on a provisional basis any relief which it would have power to grant in a final award.

(2) This includes, for instance, making—

(a) a provisional order for the payment of money or the disposition of property as between the parties, or

(b) an order to make an interim payment on account of the costs of the arbitration.

(3) Any such order shall be subject to the tribunal's final adjudication; and the tribunal's final award, on the merits or as to costs, shall take account of any such order.

(4) Unless the parties agree to confer such power on the tribunal, the tribunal has no such power.

This does not affect its powers under section 47 (awards on different issues, &c.).

40 General duty of parties

(1) The parties shall do all things necessary for the proper and expeditious conduct of the arbitral proceedings.

(2) This includes—

(a) complying without delay with any determination of the tribunal as to procedural or evidential matters, or with any order or directions of the tribunal, and

(b) where appropriate, taking without delay any necessary steps to obtain a decision of the court on a preliminary question of jurisdiction or law (see sections 32 and 45).

41 Powers of tribunal in case of party's default

(1) The parties are free to agree on the powers of the tribunal in case of a party's failure to do something necessary for the proper and expeditious conduct of the arbitration.

(2) Unless otherwise agreed by the parties, the following provisions apply.

(3) If the tribunal is satisfied that there has been inordinate and inexcusable delay on the part of the claimant in pursuing his claim and that the delay—

(a) gives rise, or is likely to give rise, to a substantial risk that it is not possible to have a fair resolution of the issues in that claim, or

(b) has caused, or is likely to cause, serious prejudice to the respondent,

the tribunal may make an award dismissing the claim.

(4) If without showing sufficient cause a party—

(a) fails to attend or be represented at an oral hearing of which due notice was given, or

(b) where matters are to be dealt with in writing, fails after due notice to submit written evidence or make written submissions,

the tribunal may continue the proceedings in the absence of that party or, as the case may be, without any written evidence or submissions on his behalf, and may make an award on the basis of the evidence before it.

(5) If without showing sufficient cause a party fails to comply with any order or directions of the tribunal, the tribunal may make a peremptory order to the same effect, prescribing such time for compliance with it as the tribunal considers appropriate.

(6) If a claimant fails to comply with a peremptory order of the tribunal to provide security for costs, the tribunal may make an award dismissing his claim.

(7) If a party fails to comply with any other kind of peremptory order, then, without prejudice to section 42 (enforcement by court of tribunal's peremptory orders), the tribunal may do any of the following—

(a) direct that the party in default shall not be entitled to rely upon any allegation or material which was the subject matter of the order;

(b) draw such adverse inferences from the act of non-compliance as the circumstances justify;

(c) proceed to an award on the basis of such materials as have been properly provided to it;
(d) make such order as it thinks fit as to the payment of costs of the arbitration incurred in consequence of the non-compliance.

Powers of court in relation to arbitral proceedings

42 Enforcement of peremptory orders of tribunal

(1) Unless otherwise agreed by the parties, the court may make an order requiring a party to comply with a peremptory order made by the tribunal.

(2) An application for an order under this section may be made—
(a) by the tribunal (upon notice to the parties),
(b) by a party to the arbitral proceedings with the permission of the tribunal (and upon notice to the other parties), or
(c) where the parties have agreed that the powers of the court under this section shall be available.

(3) The court shall not act unless it is satisfied that the applicant has exhausted any available arbitral process in respect of failure to comply with the tribunal's order.

(4) No order shall be made under this section unless the court is satisfied that the person to whom the tribunal's order was directed has failed to comply with it within the time prescribed in the order or, if no time was prescribed, within a reasonable time.

(5) The leave of the court is required for any appeal from a decision of the court under this section.

43 Securing the attendance of witnesses

(1) A party to arbitral proceedings may use the same court procedures as are available in relation to legal proceedings to secure the attendance before the tribunal of a witness in order to give oral testimony or to produce documents or other material evidence.

(2) This may only be done with the permission of the tribunal or the agreement of the other parties.

(3) The court procedures may only be used if—
(a) the witness is in the United Kingdom, and
(b) the arbitral proceedings are being conducted in England and Wales or, as the case may be, Northern Ireland.

(4) A person shall not be compelled by virtue of this section to produce any document or other material evidence which he could not be compelled to produce in legal proceedings.

44 Court powers exercisable in support of arbitral proceedings

(1) Unless otherwise agreed by the parties, the court has for the purposes of and in relation to arbitral proceedings the same power of making orders about the matters listed below as it has for the purposes of and in relation to legal proceedings.

(2) Those matters are—

(a) the taking of the evidence of witnesses;

(b) the preservation of evidence;

(c) making orders relating to property which is the subject of the proceedings or as to which any question arises in the proceedings—

(i) for the inspection, photographing, preservation, custody or detention of the property, or

(ii) ordering that samples be taken from, or any observation be made of or experiment conducted upon, the property;

and for that purpose authorising any person to enter any premises in the possession or control of a party to the arbitration;

(d) the sale of any goods the subject of the proceedings;

(e) the granting of an interim injunction or the appointment of a receiver.

(3) If the case is one of urgency, the court may, on the application of a party or proposed party to the arbitral proceedings, make such orders as it thinks necessary for the purpose of preserving evidence or assets.

(4) If the case is not one of urgency, the court shall act only on the application of a party to the arbitral proceedings (upon notice to the other parties and to the tribunal) made with the permission of the tribunal or the agreement in writing of the other parties.

(5) In any case the court shall act only if or to the extent that the arbitral tribunal, and any arbitral or other institution or person vested by the parties with power in that regard, has no power or is unable for the time being to act effectively.

(6) If the court so orders, an order made by it under this section shall cease to have effect in whole or in part on the order of the tribunal or of any such arbitral or other institution or person having power to act in relation to the subject-matter of the order.

(7) The leave of the court is required for any appeal from a decision of the court under this section.

45 Determination of preliminary point of law

(1) Unless otherwise agreed by the parties, the court may on the application of a party to arbitral proceedings (upon notice to the other parties) determine any question of law arising in the course of the proceedings which the court is satisfied substantially affects the rights of one or more of the parties.

An agreement to dispense with reasons for the tribunal's award shall be considered an agreement to exclude the court's jurisdiction under this section.

(2) An application under this section shall not be considered unless—

(a) it is made with the agreement of all the other parties to the proceedings, or

(b) it is made with the permission of the tribunal and the court is satisfied—

(i) that the determination of the question is likely to produce substantial savings in costs, and

(ii) that the application was made without delay.

(3) The application shall identify the question of law to be determined and, unless made with the agreement of all the other parties to the proceedings, shall state the grounds on which it is said that the question should be decided by the court.

(4) Unless otherwise agreed by the parties, the arbitral tribunal may continue the arbitral proceedings and make an award while an application to the court under this section is pending.

(5) Unless the court gives leave, no appeal lies from a decision of the court whether the conditions specified in subsection (2) are met.

(6) The decision of the court on the question of law shall be treated as a judgment of the court for the purposes of an appeal.

But no appeal lies without the leave of the court which shall not be given unless the court considers that the question is one of general importance, or is one which for some other special reason should be considered by the Court of Appeal.

The award

46 Rules applicable to substance of dispute

(1) The arbitral tribunal shall decide the dispute—

(a) in accordance with the law chosen by the parties as applicable to the substance of the dispute, or

(b) if the parties so agree, in accordance with such other considerations as are agreed by them or determined by the tribunal.

(2) For this purpose the choice of the laws of a country shall be understood to refer to the substantive laws of that country and not its conflict of laws rules.

(3) If or to the extent that there is no such choice or agreement, the tribunal shall apply the law determined by the conflict of laws rules which it considers applicable.

47 Awards on different issues, &c

(1) Unless otherwise agreed by the parties, the tribunal may make more than one award at different times on different aspects of the matters to be determined.

(2) The tribunal may, in particular, make an award relating—

(a) to an issue affecting the whole claim, or

(b) to a part only of the claims or cross-claims submitted to it for decision.

(3) If the tribunal does so, it shall specify in its award the issue, or the claim or part of a claim, which is the subject matter of the award.

48 Remedies

(1) The parties are free to agree on the powers exercisable by the arbitral tribunal as regards remedies.

(2) Unless otherwise agreed by the parties, the tribunal has the following powers.

(3) The tribunal may make a declaration as to any matter to be determined in the proceedings.

(4) The tribunal may order the payment of a sum of money, in any currency.

(5) The tribunal has the same powers as the court—

(a) to order a party to do or refrain from doing anything;

(b) to order specific performance of a contract (other than a contract relating to land);

(c) to order the rectification, setting aside or cancellation of a deed or other document.

49 Interest

(1) The parties are free to agree on the powers of the tribunal as regards the award of interest.

(2) Unless otherwise agreed by the parties the following provisions apply.

(3) The tribunal may award simple or compound interest from such dates, at such rates and with such rests as it considers meets the justice of the case—

(a) on the whole or part of any amount awarded by the tribunal, in respect of any period up to the date of the award;

(b) on the whole or part of any amount claimed in the arbitration and outstanding at the commencement of the arbitral proceedings but paid before the award was made, in respect of any period up to the date of payment.

(4) The tribunal may award simple or compound interest from the date of the award (or any later date) until payment, at such rates and with such rests as it considers meets the justice of the case, on the outstanding amount of any award (including any award of interest under subsection (3) and any award as to costs).

(5) References in this section to an amount awarded by the tribunal include an amount payable in consequence of a declaratory award by the tribunal.

(6) The above provisions do not affect any other power of the tribunal to award interest.

50 Extension of time for making award

(1) Where the time for making an award is limited by or in pursuance of the arbitration agreement, then, unless otherwise agreed by the parties, the court may in accordance with the following provisions by order extend that time.

(2) An application for an order under this section may be made—

(a) by the tribunal (upon notice to the parties), or

(b) by any party to the proceedings (upon notice to the tribunal and the other parties),

but only after exhausting any available arbitral process for obtaining an extension of time.

(3) The court shall only make an order if satisfied that a substantial injustice would otherwise be done.

(4) The court may extend the time for such period and on such terms as it thinks fit, and may do so whether or not the time previously fixed (by or under the agreement or by a previous order) has expired.

(5) The leave of the court is required for any appeal from a decision of the court under this section.

51 Settlement

(1) If during arbitral proceedings the parties settle the dispute, the following provisions apply unless otherwise agreed by the parties.

(2) The tribunal shall terminate the substantive proceedings and, if so requested by the parties and not objected to by the tribunal, shall record the settlement in the form of an agreed award.

(3) An agreed award shall state that it is an award of the tribunal and shall have the same status and effect as any other award on the merits of the case.

(4) The following provisions of this Part relating to awards (sections 52 to 58) apply to an agreed award.

(5) Unless the parties have also settled the matter of the payment of the costs of the arbitration, the provisions of this Part relating to costs (sections 59 to 65) continue to apply.

52 Form of award

(1) The parties are free to agree on the form of an award.

(2) If or to the extent that there is no such agreement, the following provisions apply.

(3) The award shall be in writing signed by all the arbitrators or all those assenting to the award.

(4) The award shall contain the reasons for the award unless it is an agreed award or the parties have agreed to dispense with reasons.

(5) The award shall state the seat of the arbitration and the date when the award is made.

53 Place where award treated as made

Unless otherwise agreed by the parties, where the seat of the arbitration is in England and Wales or Northern Ireland, any award in the proceedings shall be treated as made there, regardless of where it was signed, despatched or delivered to any of the parties.

54 Date of award

(1) Unless otherwise agreed by the parties, the tribunal may decide what is to be taken to be the date on which the award was made.

(2) In the absence of any such decision, the date of the award shall be taken to be the date on which it is signed by the arbitrator or, where more than one arbitrator signs the award, by the last of them.

55 Notification of award

(1) The parties are free to agree on the requirements as to notification of the award to the parties.

(2) If there is no such agreement, the award shall be notified to the parties by service on them of copies of the award, which shall be done without delay after the award is made.

(3) Nothing in this section affects section 56 (power to withhold award in case of non-payment).

56 Power to withhold award in case of non-payment

(1) The tribunal may refuse to deliver an award to the parties except upon full payment of the fees and expenses of the arbitrators.

(2) If the tribunal refuses on that ground to deliver an award, a party to the arbitral proceedings may (upon notice to the other parties and the tribunal) apply to the court, which may order that—

(a) the tribunal shall deliver the award on the payment into court by the applicant of the fees and expenses demanded, or such lesser amount as the court may specify,

(b) the amount of the fees and expenses properly payable shall be determined by such means and upon such terms as the court may direct, and

(c) out of the money paid into court there shall be paid out such fees and expenses as may be found to be properly payable and the balance of the money (if any) shall be paid out to the applicant.

(3) For this purpose the amount of fees and expenses properly payable is the amount the applicant is liable to pay under section 28 or any agreement relating to the payment of the arbitrators.

(4) No application to the court may be made where there is any available arbitral process for appeal or review of the amount of the fees or expenses demanded.

(5) References in this section to arbitrators include an arbitrator who has ceased to act and an umpire who has not replaced the other arbitrators.

(6) The above provisions of this section also apply in relation to any arbitral or other institution or person vested by the parties with powers in relation to the delivery of the tribunal's award.

As they so apply, the references to the fees and expenses of the arbitrators shall be construed as including the fees and expenses of that institution or person.

(7) The leave of the court is required for any appeal from a decision of the court under this section.

(8) Nothing in this section shall be construed as excluding an application under section 28 where payment has been made to the arbitrators in order to obtain the award.

57 Correction of award or additional award

(1) The parties are free to agree on the powers of the tribunal to correct an award or make an additional award.

(2) If or to the extent there is no such agreement, the following provisions apply.

(3) The tribunal may on its own initiative or on the application of a party—

(a) correct an award so as to remove any clerical mistake or error arising from an accidental slip or omission or clarify or remove any ambiguity in the award, or

(b) make an additional award in respect of any claim (including a claim for interest or costs) which was presented to the tribunal but was not dealt with in the award.

These powers shall not be exercised without first affording the other parties a reasonable opportunity to make representations to the tribunal.

(4) Any application for the exercise of those powers must be made within 28 days of the date of the award or such longer period as the parties may agree.

(5) Any correction of an award shall be made within 28 days of the date the application was received by the tribunal or, where the correction is made by the tribunal on its own initiative, within 28 days of the date of the award or, in either case, such longer period as the parties may agree.

(6) Any additional award shall be made within 56 days of the date of the original award or such longer period as the parties may agree.

(7) Any correction of an award shall form part of the award.

58 Effect of award

(1) Unless otherwise agreed by the parties, an award made by the tribunal pursuant to an arbitration agreement is final and binding both on the parties and on any persons claiming through or under them.

(2) This does not affect the right of a person to challenge the award by any available arbitral process of appeal or review or in accordance with the provisions of this Part.

Costs of the arbitration

59 Costs of the arbitration

(1) References in this Part to the costs of the arbitration are to—

(a) the arbitrators' fees and expenses,

(b) the fees and expenses of any arbitral institution concerned, and

(c) the legal or other costs of the parties.

(2) Any such reference includes the costs of or incidental to any proceedings to determine the amount of the recoverable costs of the arbitration (see section 63).

60 Agreement to pay costs in any event

An agreement which has the effect that a party is to pay the whole or part of the costs of the arbitration in any event is only valid if made after the dispute in question has arisen.

61 Award of costs

(1) The tribunal may make an award allocating the costs of the arbitration as between the parties, subject to any agreement of the parties.

(2) Unless the parties otherwise agree, the tribunal shall award costs on the general principle that costs should follow the event except where it appears to the tribunal that in the circumstances this is not appropriate in relation to the whole or part of the costs.

62 Effect of agreement or award about costs

Unless the parties otherwise agree, any obligation under an agreement between them as to how the costs of the arbitration are to be borne, or under an award allocating the costs of the arbitration, extends only to such costs as are recoverable.

63 The recoverable costs of the arbitration

(1) The parties are free to agree what costs of the arbitration are recoverable.

(2) If or to the extent there is no such agreement, the following provisions apply.

(3) The tribunal may determine by award the recoverable costs of the arbitration on such basis as it thinks fit.

If it does so, it shall specify—
- (a) the basis on which it has acted, and
- (b) the items of recoverable costs and the amount referable to each.

(4) If the tribunal does not determine the recoverable costs of the arbitration, any party to the arbitral proceedings may apply to the court (upon notice to the other parties) which may—
- (a) determine the recoverable costs of the arbitration on such basis as it thinks fit, or
- (b) order that they shall be determined by such means and upon such terms as it may specify.

(5) Unless the tribunal or the court determines otherwise—
- (a) the recoverable costs of the arbitration shall be determined on the basis that there shall be allowed a reasonable amount in respect of all costs reasonably incurred, and
- (b) any doubt as to whether costs were reasonably incurred or were reasonable in amount shall be resolved in favour of the paying party.

(6) The above provisions have effect subject to section 64 (recoverable fees and expenses of arbitrators).

(7) Nothing in this section affects any right of the arbitrators, any expert, legal adviser or assessor appointed by the tribunal, or any arbitral institution, to payment of their fees and expenses.

64 Recoverable fees and expenses of arbitrators

(1) Unless otherwise agreed by the parties, the recoverable costs of the arbitration shall include in respect of the fees and expenses of the arbitrators only such reasonable fees and expenses as are appropriate in the circumstances.

(2) If there is any question as to what reasonable fees and expenses are appropriate in the circumstances, and the matter is not already before the court on an application under section 63(4), the court may on the application of any party (upon notice to the other parties)—

(a) determine the matter, or

(b) order that it be determined by such means and upon such terms as the court may specify.

(3) Subsection (1) has effect subject to any order of the court under section 24(4) or 25(3)(b) (order as to entitlement to fees or expenses in case of removal or resignation of arbitrator).

(4) Nothing in this section affects any right of the arbitrator to payment of his fees and expenses.

65 Power to limit recoverable costs

(1) Unless otherwise agreed by the parties, the tribunal may direct that the recoverable costs of the arbitration, or of any part of the arbitral proceedings, shall be limited to a specified amount.

(2) Any direction may be made or varied at any stage, but this must be done sufficiently in advance of the incurring of costs to which it relates, or the taking of any steps in the proceedings which may be affected by it, for the limit to be taken into account.

Powers of the court in relation to award

66 Enforcement of the award

(1) An award made by the tribunal pursuant to an arbitration agreement may, by leave of the court, be enforced in the same manner as a judgment or order of the court to the same effect.

(2) Where leave is so given, judgment may be entered in terms of the award.

(3) Leave to enforce an award shall not be given where, or to the extent that, the person against whom it is sought to be enforced shows that the tribunal lacked substantive jurisdiction to make the award.

The right to raise such an objection may have been lost (see section 73).

(4) Nothing in this section affects the recognition or enforcement of an award under any other enactment or rule of law, in particular under Part II of the Arbitration Act 1950 (enforcement of awards under Geneva Convention) or the provisions of Part III of this Act relating to the recognition and enforcement of awards under the New York Convention or by an action on the award.

67 Challenging the award: substantive jurisdiction

(1) A party to arbitral proceedings may (upon notice to the other parties and to the tribunal) apply to the court—

(a) challenging any award of the arbitral tribunal as to its substantive jurisdiction; or

(b) for an order declaring an award made by the tribunal on the merits to be of no effect, in whole or in part, because the tribunal did not have substantive jurisdiction.

A party may lose the right to object (see section 73) and the right to apply is subject to the restrictions in section 70(2) and (3).

(2) The arbitral tribunal may continue the arbitral proceedings and make a further award while an application to the court under this section is pending in relation to an award as to jurisdiction.

(3) On an application under this section challenging an award of the arbitral tribunal as to its substantive jurisdiction, the court may by order—

(a) confirm the award,

(b) vary the award, or

(c) set aside the award in whole or in part.

(4) The leave of the court is required for any appeal from a decision of the court under this section.

68 Challenging the award: serious irregularity

(1) A party to arbitral proceedings may (upon notice to the other parties and to the tribunal) apply to the court challenging an award in the proceedings on the ground of serious irregularity affecting the tribunal, the proceedings or the award.

A party may lose the right to object (see section 73) and the right to apply is subject to the restrictions in section 70(2) and (3).

(2) Serious irregularity means an irregularity of one or more of the following kinds which the court considers has caused or will cause substantial injustice to the applicant—

(a) failure by the tribunal to comply with section 33 (general duty of tribunal);

(b) the tribunal exceeding its powers (otherwise than by exceeding its substantive jurisdiction: see section 67);

(c) failure by the tribunal to conduct the proceedings in accordance with the procedure agreed by the parties;

(d) failure by the tribunal to deal with all the issues that were put to it;

(e) any arbitral or other institution or person vested by the parties with powers in relation to the proceedings or the award exceeding its powers;

(f) uncertainty or ambiguity as to the effect of the award;

(g) the award being obtained by fraud or the award or the way in which it was procured being contrary to public policy;

(h) failure to comply with the requirements as to the form of the award; or

(i) any irregularity in the conduct of the proceedings or in the award which is admitted by the tribunal or by any arbitral or other institution or person vested by the parties with powers in relation to the proceedings or the award.

(3) If there is shown to be serious irregularity affecting the tribunal, the proceedings or the award, the court may—

(a) remit the award to the tribunal, in whole or in part, for reconsideration,

(b) set the award aside in whole or in part, or

(c) declare the award to be of no effect, in whole or in part.

The court shall not exercise its power to set aside or to declare an award to be of no effect, in whole or in part, unless it is satisfied that it would be inappropriate to remit the matters in question to the tribunal for reconsideration.

(4) The leave of the court is required for any appeal from a decision of the court under this section.

69 Appeal on point of law

(1) Unless otherwise agreed by the parties, a party to arbitral proceedings may (upon notice to the other parties and to the tribunal) appeal to the court on a question of law arising out of an award made in the proceedings.

An agreement to dispense with reasons for the tribunal's award shall be considered an agreement to exclude the court's jurisdiction under this section.

(2) An appeal shall not be brought under this section except—

(a) with the agreement of all the other parties to the proceedings, or

(b) with the leave of the court.

The right to appeal is also subject to the restrictions in section 70(2) and (3).

(3) Leave to appeal shall be given only if the court is satisfied—

(a) that the determination of the question will substantially affect the rights of one or more of the parties,

(b) that the question is one which the tribunal was asked to determine,

(c) that, on the basis of the findings of fact in the award—

(i) the decision of the tribunal on the question is obviously wrong, or

(ii) the question is one of general public importance and the decision of the tribunal is at least open to serious doubt, and

(d) that, despite the agreement of the parties to resolve the matter by arbitration, it is just and proper in all the circumstances for the court to determine the question.

(4) An application for leave to appeal under this section shall identify the question of law to be determined and state the grounds on which it is alleged that leave to appeal should be granted.

(5) The court shall determine an application for leave to appeal under this section without a hearing unless it appears to the court that a hearing is required.

(6) The leave of the court is required for any appeal from a decision of the court under this section to grant or refuse leave to appeal.

(7) On an appeal under this section the court may by order—

(a) confirm the award,

(b) vary the award,

(c) remit the award to the tribunal, in whole or in part, for reconsideration in the light of the court's determination, or
(d) set aside the award in whole or in part.

The court shall not exercise its power to set aside an award, in whole or in part, unless it is satisfied that it would be inappropriate to remit the matters in question to the tribunal for reconsideration.

(8) The decision of the court on an appeal under this section shall be treated as a judgment of the court for the purposes of a further appeal.

But no such appeal lies without the leave of the court which shall not be given unless the court considers that the question is one of general importance or is one which for some other special reason should be considered by the Court of Appeal.

70 Challenge or appeal: supplementary provisions

(1) The following provisions apply to an application or appeal under section 67, 68 or 69.

(2) An application or appeal may not be brought if the applicant or appellant has not first exhausted—
(a) any available arbitral process of appeal or review, and
(b) any available recourse under section 57 (correction of award or additional award).

(3) Any application or appeal must be brought within 28 days of the date of the award or, if there has been any arbitral process of appeal or review, of the date when the applicant or appellant was notified of the result of that process.

(4) If on an application or appeal it appears to the court that the award—
(a) does not contain the tribunal's reasons, or
(b) does not set out the tribunal's reasons in sufficient detail to enable the court properly to consider the application or appeal,

the court may order the tribunal to state the reasons for its award in sufficient detail for that purpose.

(5) Where the court makes an order under subsection (4), it may make such further order as it thinks fit with respect to any additional costs of the arbitration resulting from its order.

(6) The court may order the applicant or appellant to provide security for the costs of the application or appeal, and may direct that the application or appeal be dismissed if the order is not complied with.

The power to order security for costs shall not be exercised on the ground that the applicant or appellant is—
(a) an individual ordinarily resident outside the United Kingdom, or
(b) a corporation or association incorporated or formed under the law of a country outside the United Kingdom, or whose central management and control is exercised outside the United Kingdom.

(7) The court may order that any money payable under the award shall be brought into court or otherwise secured pending the determination of the application or appeal, and may direct that the application or appeal be dismissed if the order is not complied with.

(8) The court may grant leave to appeal subject to conditions to the same or similar effect as an order under subsection (6) or (7).

This does not affect the general discretion of the court to grant leave subject to conditions.

71 Challenge or appeal: effect of order of court

(1) The following provisions have effect where the court makes an order under section 67, 68 or 69 with respect to an award.

(2) Where the award is varied, the variation has effect as part of the tribunal's award.

(3) Where the award is remitted to the tribunal, in whole or in part, for reconsideration, the tribunal shall make a fresh award in respect of the matters remitted within three months of the date of the order for remission or such longer or shorter period as the court may direct.

(4) Where the award is set aside or declared to be of no effect, in whole or in part, the court may also order that any provision that an award is a condition precedent to the bringing of legal proceedings in respect of a matter to which the arbitration agreement applies, is of no effect as regards the subject matter of the award or, as the case may be, the relevant part of the award.

Miscellaneous

72 Saving for rights of person who takes no part in proceedings

(1) A person alleged to be a party to arbitral proceedings but who takes no part in the proceedings may question—

(a) whether there is a valid arbitration agreement,

(b) whether the tribunal is properly constituted, or

(c) what matters have been submitted to arbitration in accordance with the arbitration agreement,

by proceedings in the court for a declaration or injunction or other appropriate relief.

(2) He also has the same right as a party to the arbitral proceedings to challenge an award—

(a) by an application under section 67 on the ground of lack of substantive jurisdiction in relation to him, or

(b) by an application under section 68 on the ground of serious irregularity (within the meaning of that section) affecting him;

and section 70(2) (duty to exhaust arbitral procedures) does not apply in his case.

73 Loss of right to object

(1) If a party to arbitral proceedings takes part, or continues to take part, in the proceedings without making, either forthwith or within such time as is allowed by the arbitration agreement or the tribunal or by any provision of this Part, any objection—

(a) that the tribunal lacks substantive jurisdiction,

(b) that the proceedings have been improperly conducted,

(c) that there has been a failure to comply with the arbitration agreement or with any provision of this Part, or

(d) that there has been any other irregularity affecting the tribunal or the proceedings,

he may not raise that objection later, before the tribunal or the court, unless he shows that, at the time he took part or continued to take part in the proceedings, he did not know and could not with reasonable diligence have discovered the grounds for the objection.

(2) Where the arbitral tribunal rules that it has substantive jurisdiction and a party to arbitral proceedings who could have questioned that ruling—

(a) by any available arbitral process of appeal or review, or

(b) by challenging the award,

does not do so, or does not do so within the time allowed by the arbitration agreement or any provision of this Part, he may not object later to the tribunal's substantive jurisdiction on any ground which was the subject of that ruling.

74 Immunity of arbitral institutions, &c

(1) An arbitral or other institution or person designated or requested by the parties to appoint or nominate an arbitrator is not liable for anything done or omitted in the discharge or purported discharge of that function unless the act or omission is shown to have been in bad faith.

(2) An arbitral or other institution or person by whom an arbitrator is appointed or nominated is not liable, by reason of having appointed or nominated him, for anything done or omitted by the arbitrator (or his employees or agents) in the discharge or purported discharge of his functions as arbitrator.

(3) The above provisions apply to an employee or agent of an arbitral or other institution or person as they apply to the institution or person himself.

75 Charge to secure payment of solicitors' costs

The powers of the court to make declarations and orders under section 73 of the Solicitors Act 1974 or Article 71H of the Solicitors (Northern Ireland) Order 1976 (power to charge property recovered in the proceedings with the payment of solicitors' costs) may be exercised in relation to arbitral proceedings as if those proceedings were proceedings in the court.

Supplementary

76 Service of notices, &c

(1) The parties are free to agree on the manner of service of any notice or other document required or authorised to be given or served in pursuance of the arbitration agreement or for the purposes of the arbitral proceedings.

(2) If or to the extent that there is no such agreement the following provisions apply.

(3) A notice or other document may be served on a person by any effective means.

(4) If a notice or other document is addressed, pre-paid and delivered by post—

(a) to the addressee's last known principal residence or, if he is or has been carrying on a trade, profession or business, his last known principal business address, or

(b) where the addressee is a body corporate, to the body's registered or principal office,

it shall be treated as effectively served.

(5) This section does not apply to the service of documents for the purposes of legal proceedings, for which provision is made by rules of court.

(6) References in this Part to a notice or other document include any form of communication in writing and references to giving or serving a notice or other document shall be construed accordingly.

77 Powers of court in relation to service of documents

(1) This section applies where service of a document on a person in the manner agreed by the parties, or in accordance with provisions of section 76 having effect in default of agreement, is not reasonably practicable.

(2) Unless otherwise agreed by the parties, the court may make such order as it thinks fit—

(a) for service in such manner as the court may direct, or

(b) dispensing with service of the document.

(3) Any party to the arbitration agreement may apply for an order, but only after exhausting any available arbitral process for resolving the matter.

(4) The leave of the court is required for any appeal from a decision of the court under this section.

78 Reckoning periods of time

(1) The parties are free to agree on the method of reckoning periods of time for the purposes of any provision agreed by them or any provision of this Part having effect in default of such agreement.

(2) If or to the extent there is no such agreement, periods of time shall be reckoned in accordance with the following provisions.

(3) Where the act is required to be done within a specified period after or from a specified date, the period begins immediately after that date.

(4) Where the act is required to be done a specified number of clear days after a specified date, at least that number of days must intervene between the day on which the act is done and that date.

(5) Where the period is a period of seven days or less which would include a Saturday, Sunday or a public holiday in the place where anything which has to be done within the period falls to be done, that day shall be excluded.

In relation to England and Wales or Northern Ireland, a "public holiday" means Christmas Day, Good Friday or a day which under the Banking and Financial Dealings Act 1971 is a bank holiday.

79 Power of court to extend time limits relating to arbitral proceedings

(1) Unless the parties otherwise agree, the court may by order extend any time limit agreed by them in relation to any matter relating to the arbitral proceedings or specified in any provision of this Part having effect in default of such agreement.

This section does not apply to a time limit to which section 12 applies (power of court to extend time for beginning arbitral proceedings, &c.).

(2) An application for an order may be made—

(a) by any party to the arbitral proceedings (upon notice to the other parties and to the tribunal), or

(b) by the arbitral tribunal (upon notice to the parties).

(3) The court shall not exercise its power to extend a time limit unless it is satisfied—

(a) that any available recourse to the tribunal, or to any arbitral or other institution or person vested by the parties with power in that regard, has first been exhausted, and

(b) that a substantial injustice would otherwise be done.

(4) The court's power under this section may be exercised whether or not the time has already expired.

(5) An order under this section may be made on such terms as the court thinks fit.

(6) The leave of the court is required for any appeal from a decision of the court under this section.

80 Notice and other requirements in connection with legal proceedings

(1) References in this Part to an application, appeal or other step in relation to legal proceedings being taken "upon notice" to the other parties to the arbitral proceedings, or to the tribunal, are to such notice of the originating process as is required by rules of court and do not impose any separate requirement.

(2) Rules of court shall be made—

(a) requiring such notice to be given as indicated by any provision of this Part, and

(b) as to the manner, form and content of any such notice.

(3) Subject to any provision made by rules of court, a requirement to give notice to the tribunal of legal proceedings shall be construed—

(a) if there is more than one arbitrator, as a requirement to give notice to each of them; and

(b) if the tribunal is not fully constituted, as a requirement to give notice to any arbitrator who has been appointed.

(4) References in this Part to making an application or appeal to the court within a specified period are to the issue within that period of the appropriate originating process in accordance with rules of court.

(5) Where any provision of this Part requires an application or appeal to be made to the court within a specified time, the rules of court relating to the reckoning of periods, the extending or abridging of periods, and the consequences of not taking a step within the period prescribed by the rules, apply in relation to that requirement.

(6) Provision may be made by rules of court amending the provisions of this Part—

(a) with respect to the time within which any application or appeal to the court must be made,

(b) so as to keep any provision made by this Part in relation to arbitral proceedings in step with the corresponding provision of rules of court applying in relation to proceedings in the court, or

(c) so as to keep any provision made by this Part in relation to legal proceedings in step with the corresponding provision of rules of court applying generally in relation to proceedings in the court.

(7) Nothing in this section affects the generality of the power to make rules of court.

81 Saving for certain matters governed by common law

(1) Nothing in this Part shall be construed as excluding the operation of any rule of law consistent with the provisions of this Part, in particular, any rule of law as to—

(a) matters which are not capable of settlement by arbitration;

(b) the effect of an oral arbitration agreement; or

(c) the refusal of recognition or enforcement of an arbitral award on grounds of public policy.

(2) Nothing in this Act shall be construed as reviving any jurisdiction of the court to set aside or remit an award on the ground of errors of fact or law on the face of the award.

82 Minor definitions

(1) In this Part—

"arbitrator", unless the context otherwise requires, includes an umpire;

"available arbitral process", in relation to any matter, includes any process of appeal to or review by an arbitral or other institution or person vested by the parties with powers in relation to that matter;

"claimant", unless the context otherwise requires, includes a counterclaimant, and related expressions shall be construed accordingly;

"dispute" includes any difference;

"enactment" includes an enactment contained in Northern Ireland legislation;

"legal proceedings" means civil proceedings in the High Court or a county court;

"peremptory order" means an order made under section 41(5) or made in exercise of any corresponding power conferred by the parties;

"premises" includes land, buildings, moveable structures, vehicles, vessels, aircraft and hovercraft;

"question of law" means—

(a) for a court in England and Wales, a question of the law of England and Wales, and

(b) for a court in Northern Ireland, a question of the law of Northern Ireland;

"substantive jurisdiction", in relation to an arbitral tribunal, refers to the matters specified in section 30(1)(a) to (c), and references to the tribunal exceeding its substantive jurisdiction shall be construed accordingly.

(2) References in this Part to a party to an arbitration agreement include any person claiming under or through a party to the agreement.

83 Index of defined expressions: Part I

In this Part the expressions listed below are defined or otherwise explained by the provisions indicated—

agreement, agree and agreed	section 5(1)
agreement in writing	section 5(2) to (5)
arbitration agreement	sections 6 and 5(1)
arbitrator	section 82(1)
available arbitral process	section 82(1)
claimant	section 82(1)
commencement (in relation to arbitral proceedings)	section 14
costs of the arbitration	section 59
the court	section 105
dispute	section 82(1)
enactment	section 82(1)
legal proceedings	section 82(1)
Limitation Acts	section 13(4)
notice (or other document)	section 76(6)
party—	
—in relation to an arbitration agreement	section 82(2)
—where section 106(2) or (3) applies	section 106(4)
peremptory order	section 82(1) (and see section 41(5))
premises	section 82(1)
question of law	section 82(1)
recoverable costs	sections 63 and 64
seat of the arbitration	section 3
serve and service (of notice or other document)	section 76(6)
substantive jurisdiction (in relation to an arbitral tribunal)	section 82(1) (and see section 30(1)(a) to (c))
upon notice (to the parties or the tribunal)	section 80
written and in writing	section 5(6)

84 Transitional provisions

(1) The provisions of this Part do not apply to arbitral proceedings commenced before the date on which this Part comes into force.

(2) They apply to arbitral proceedings commenced on or after that date under an arbitration agreement whenever made.

(3) The above provisions have effect subject to any transitional provision made by an order under section 109(2) (power to include transitional provisions in commencement order).

PART II

OTHER PROVISIONS RELATING TO ARBITRATION

Domestic arbitration agreements

85 Modification of Part I in relation to domestic arbitration agreement

(1) In the case of a domestic arbitration agreement the provisions of Part I are modified in accordance with the following sections.

(2) For this purpose a "domestic arbitration agreement" means an arbitration agreement to which none of the parties is—

(a) an individual who is a national of, or habitually resident in, a state other than the United Kingdom, or

(b) a body corporate which is incorporated in, or whose central control and management is exercised in, a state other than the United Kingdom,

and under which the seat of the arbitration (if the seat has been designated or determined) is in the United Kingdom.

(3) In subsection (2) "arbitration agreement" and "seat of the arbitration" have the same meaning as in Part I (see sections 3, 5(1) and 6).

86 Staying of legal proceedings

(1) In section 9 (stay of legal proceedings), subsection (4) (stay unless the arbitration agreement is null and void, inoperative, or incapable of being performed) does not apply to a domestic arbitration agreement.

(2) On an application under that section in relation to a domestic arbitration agreement the court shall grant a stay unless satisfied—

(a) that the arbitration agreement is null and void, inoperative, or incapable of being performed, or

(b) that there are other sufficient grounds for not requiring the parties to abide by the arbitration agreement.

(3) The court may treat as a sufficient ground under subsection (2)(b) the fact that the applicant is or was at any material time not ready and willing to do all things necessary for the proper conduct of the arbitration or of any other dispute resolution procedures required to be exhausted before resorting to arbitration.

(4) For the purposes of this section the question whether an arbitration agreement is a domestic arbitration agreement shall be determined by reference to the facts at the time the legal proceedings are commenced.

87 Effectiveness of agreement to exclude court's jurisdiction

(1) In the case of a domestic arbitration agreement any agreement to exclude the jurisdiction of the court under—

(a) section 45 (determination of preliminary point of law), or

(b) section 69 (challenging the award: appeal on point of law),

is not effective unless entered into after the commencement of the arbitral proceedings in which the question arises or the award is made.

(2) For this purpose the commencement of the arbitral proceedings has the same meaning as in Part I (see section 14).

(3) For the purposes of this section the question whether an arbitration agreement is a domestic arbitration agreement shall be determined by reference to the facts at the time the agreement is entered into.

88 Power to repeal or amend sections 85 to 87

(1) The Secretary of State may by order repeal or amend the provisions of sections 85 to 87.

(2) An order under this section may contain such supplementary, incidental and transitional provisions as appear to the Secretary of State to be appropriate.

(3) An order under this section shall be made by statutory instrument and no such order shall be made unless a draft of it has been laid before and approved by a resolution of each House of Parliament.

Consumer arbitration agreements

89 Application of unfair terms regulations to consumer arbitration agreements

(1) The following sections extend the application of the Unfair Terms in Consumer Contracts Regulations 1994 in relation to a term which constitutes an arbitration agreement.

For this purpose "arbitration agreement" means an agreement to submit to arbitration present or future disputes or differences (whether or not contractual).

(2) In those sections "the Regulations" means those regulations and includes any regulations amending or replacing those regulations.

(3) Those sections apply whatever the law applicable to the arbitration agreement.

90 Regulations apply where consumer is a legal person

The Regulations apply where the consumer is a legal person as they apply where the consumer is a natural person.

91 Arbitration agreement unfair where modest amount sought

(1) A term which constitutes an arbitration agreement is unfair for the purposes of the Regulations so far as it relates to a claim for a pecuniary remedy which does not exceed the amount specified by order for the purposes of this section.

(2) Orders under this section may make different provision for different cases and for different purposes.

(3) The power to make orders under this section is exercisable—

(a) for England and Wales, by the Secretary of State with the concurrence of the Lord Chancellor,

(b) for Scotland, by the Secretary of State with the concurrence of the Lord Advocate, and

(c) for Northern Ireland, by the Department of Economic Development for Northern Ireland with the concurrence of the Lord Chancellor.

(4) Any such order for England and Wales or Scotland shall be made by statutory instrument which shall be subject to annulment in pursuance of a resolution of either House of Parliament.

(5) Any such order for Northern Ireland shall be a statutory rule for the purposes of the Statutory Rules (Northern Ireland) Order 1979 and shall be subject to negative resolution, within the meaning of section 41(6) of the Interpretation Act (Northern Ireland) 1954.

Small claims arbitration in the county court

92 Exclusion of Part I in relation to small claims arbitration in the county court

Nothing in Part I of this Act applies to arbitration under section 64 of the County Courts Act 1984.

Appointment of judges as arbitrators

93 Appointment of judges as arbitrators

(1) A judge of the Commercial Court or an official referee may, if in all the circumstances he thinks fit, accept appointment as a sole arbitrator or as umpire by or by virtue of an arbitration agreement.

(2) A judge of the Commercial Court shall not do so unless the Lord Chief Justice has informed him that, having regard to the state of business in the High Court and the Crown Court, he can be made available.

(3) An official referee shall not do so unless the Lord Chief Justice has informed him that, having regard to the state of official referees' business, he can be made available.

(4) The fees payable for the services of a judge of the Commercial Court or official referee as arbitrator or umpire shall be taken in the High Court.

(5) In this section—

"arbitration agreement" has the same meaning as in Part I; and "official referee" means a person nominated under section 68(1)(a) of the Supreme Court Act 1981 to deal with official referees' business.

(6) The provisions of Part I of this Act apply to arbitration before a person appointed under this section with the modifications specified in Schedule 2.

Statutory arbitrations

94 Application of Part I to statutory arbitrations

(1) The provisions of Part I apply to every arbitration under an enactment (a "statutory arbitration"), whether the enactment was passed or made before or after the commencement of this Act, subject to the adaptations and exclusions specified in sections 95 to 98.

(2) The provisions of Part I do not apply to a statutory arbitration if or to the extent that their application—

(a) is inconsistent with the provisions of the enactment concerned, with any rules or procedure authorised or recognised by it, or

(b) is excluded by any other enactment.

(3) In this section and the following provisions of this Part "enactment"—

(a) in England and Wales, includes an enactment contained in subordinate legislation within the meaning of the Interpretation Act 1978;

(b) in Northern Ireland, means a statutory provision within the meaning of section 1(f) of the Interpretation Act (Northern Ireland) 1954.

95 General adaptation of provisions in relation to statutory arbitrations

(1) The provisions of Part I apply to a statutory arbitration—

(a) as if the arbitration were pursuant to an arbitration agreement and as if the enactment were that agreement, and

(b) as if the persons by and against whom a claim subject to arbitration in pursuance of the enactment may be or has been made were parties to that agreement.

(2) Every statutory arbitration shall be taken to have its seat in England and Wales or, as the case may be, in Northern Ireland.

96 Specific adaptations of provisions in relation to statutory arbitrations

(1) The following provisions of Part I apply to a statutory arbitration with the following adaptations.

(2) In section 30(1) (competence of tribunal to rule on its own jurisdiction), the reference in paragraph (a) to whether there is a valid arbitration agreement shall be construed as a reference to whether the enactment applies to the dispute or difference in question.

(3) Section 35 (consolidation of proceedings and concurrent hearings) applies only so as to authorise the consolidation of proceedings, or concurrent hearings in proceedings, under the same enactment.

(4) Section 46 (rules applicable to substance of dispute) applies with the omission of subsection (1)(b) (determination in accordance with considerations agreed by parties).

97 Provisions excluded from applying to statutory arbitrations

The following provisions of Part I do not apply in relation to a statutory arbitration—

- (a) section 8 (whether agreement discharged by death of a party);
- (b) section 12 (power of court to extend agreed time limits);
- (c) sections 9(5), 10(2) and 71(4) (restrictions on effect of provision that award condition precedent to right to bring legal proceedings).

98 Power to make further provision by regulations

(1) The Secretary of State may make provision by regulations for adapting or excluding any provision of Part I in relation to statutory arbitrations in general or statutory arbitrations of any particular description.

(2) The power is exercisable whether the enactment concerned is passed or made before or after the commencement of this Act.

(3) Regulations under this section shall be made by statutory instrument which shall be subject to annulment in pursuance of a resolution of either House of Parliament.

PART III

RECOGNITION AND ENFORCEMENT OF CERTAIN FOREIGN AWARDS

Enforcement of Geneva Convention awards

99 Continuation of Part II of the Arbitration Act 1950

Part II of the Arbitration Act 1950 (enforcement of certain foreign awards) continues to apply in relation to foreign awards within the meaning of that Part which are not also New York Convention awards.

Recognition and enforcement of New York Convention awards

100 New York Convention awards

(1) In this Part a "New York Convention award" means an award made, in pursuance of an arbitration agreement, in the territory of a state (other than the United Kingdom) which is a party to the New York Convention.

(2) For the purposes of subsection (1) and of the provisions of this Part relating to such awards—

- (a) "arbitration agreement" means an arbitration agreement in writing, and
- (b) an award shall be treated as made at the seat of the arbitration, regardless of where it was signed, despatched or delivered to any of the parties.

In this subsection "agreement in writing" and "seat of the arbitration" have the same meaning as in Part I.

(3) If Her Majesty by Order in Council declares that a state specified in the Order is a party to the New York Convention, or is a party in respect of any territory so specified, the Order shall, while in force, be conclusive evidence of that fact.

(4) In this section "the New York Convention" means the Convention on the Recognition and Enforcement of Foreign Arbitral Awards adopted by the United Nations Conference on International Commercial Arbitration on 10th June 1958.

101 Recognition and enforcement of awards

(1) A New York Convention award shall be recognised as binding on the persons as between whom it was made, and may accordingly be relied on by those persons by way of defence, set-off or otherwise in any legal proceedings in England and Wales or Northern Ireland.

(2) A New York Convention award may, by leave of the court, be enforced in the same manner as a judgment or order of the court to the same effect.

As to the meaning of "the court" see section 105.

(3) Where leave is so given, judgment may be entered in terms of the award.

102 Evidence to be produced by party seeking recognition or enforcement

(1) A party seeking the recognition or enforcement of a New York Convention award must produce—

(a) the duly authenticated original award or a duly certified copy of it, and

(b) the original arbitration agreement or a duly certified copy of it.

(2) If the award or agreement is in a foreign language, the party must also produce a translation of it certified by an official or sworn translator or by a diplomatic or consular agent.

103 Refusal of recognition or enforcement

(1) Recognition or enforcement of a New York Convention award shall not be refused except in the following cases.

(2) Recognition or enforcement of the award may be refused if the person against whom it is invoked proves—

(a) that a party to the arbitration agreement was (under the law applicable to him) under some incapacity;

(b) that the arbitration agreement was not valid under the law to which the parties subjected it or, failing any indication thereon, under the law of the country where the award was made;

(c) that he was not given proper notice of the appointment of the arbitrator or of the arbitration proceedings or was otherwise unable to present his case;

(d) that the award deals with a difference not contemplated by or not falling within the terms of the submission to arbitration or contains decisions on matters beyond the scope of the submission to arbitration (but see subsection (4));

(e) that the composition of the arbitral tribunal or the arbitral procedure was not in accordance with the agreement of the parties or, failing such agreement, with the law of the country in which the arbitration took place;

(f) that the award has not yet become binding on the parties, or has been set aside or suspended by a competent authority of the country in which, or under the law of which, it was made.

(3) Recognition or enforcement of the award may also be refused if the award is in respect of a matter which is not capable of settlement by arbitration, or if it would be contrary to public policy to recognise or enforce the award.

(4) An award which contains decisions on matters not submitted to arbitration may be recognised or enforced to the extent that it contains decisions on matters submitted to arbitration which can be separated from those on matters not so submitted.

(5) Where an application for the setting aside or suspension of the award has been made to such a competent authority as is mentioned in subsection (2)(f), the court before which the award is sought to be relied upon may, if it considers it proper, adjourn the decision on the recognition or enforcement of the award.

It may also on the application of the party claiming recognition or enforcement of the award order the other party to give suitable security.

104 Saving for other bases of recognition or enforcement

Nothing in the preceding provisions of this Part affects any right to rely upon or enforce a New York Convention award at common law or under section 66.

PART IV

GENERAL PROVISIONS

105 Meaning of "the court": jurisdiction of High Court and county court

(1) In this Act "the court" means the High Court or a county court, subject to the following provisions.

(2) The Lord Chancellor may by order make provision—

(a) allocating proceedings under this Act to the High Court or to county courts; or

(b) specifying proceedings under this Act which may be commenced or taken only in the High Court or in a county court.

(3) The Lord Chancellor may by order make provision requiring proceedings of any specified description under this Act in relation to which a county court has jurisdiction to be commenced or taken in one or more specified county courts.

Any jurisdiction so exercisable by a specified county court is exercisable throughout England and Wales or, as the case may be, Northern Ireland.

(4) An order under this section—

(a) may differentiate between categories of proceedings by reference to such criteria as the Lord Chancellor sees fit to specify, and

(b) may make such incidental or transitional provision as the Lord Chancellor considers necessary or expedient.

(5) An order under this section for England and Wales shall be made by statutory instrument which shall be subject to annulment in pursuance of a resolution of either House of Parliament.

(6) An order under this section for Northern Ireland shall be a statutory rule for the purposes of the Statutory Rules (Northern Ireland) Order 1979 which shall be subject to annulment in pursuance of a resolution of either House of Parliament in like manner as a statutory instrument and section 5 of the Statutory Instruments Act 1946 shall apply accordingly.

106 Crown application

(1) Part I of this Act applies to any arbitration agreement to which Her Majesty, either in right of the Crown or of the Duchy of Lancaster or otherwise, or the Duke of Cornwall, is a party.

(2) Where Her Majesty is party to an arbitration agreement otherwise than in right of the Crown, Her Majesty shall be represented for the purposes of any arbitral proceedings—

(a) where the agreement was entered into by Her Majesty in right of the Duchy of Lancaster, by the Chancellor of the Duchy or such person as he may appoint, and

(b) in any other case, by such person as Her Majesty may appoint in writing under the Royal Sign Manual.

(3) Where the Duke of Cornwall is party to an arbitration agreement, he shall be represented for the purposes of any arbitral proceedings by such person as he may appoint.

(4) References in Part I to a party or the parties to the arbitration agreement or to arbitral proceedings shall be construed, where subsection (2) or (3) applies, as references to the person representing Her Majesty or the Duke of Cornwall.

107 Consequential amendments and repeals

(1) The enactments specified in Schedule 3 are amended in accordance with that Schedule, the amendments being consequential on the provisions of this Act.

(2) The enactments specified in Schedule 4 are repealed to the extent specified.

108 Extent

(1) The provisions of this Act extend to England and Wales and, except as mentioned below, to Northern Ireland.

(2) The following provisions of Part II do not extend to Northern Ireland—

section 92 (exclusion of Part I in relation to small claims arbitration in the county court), and

section 93 and Schedule 2 (appointment of judges as arbitrators).

(3) Sections 89, 90 and 91 (consumer arbitration agreements) extend to Scotland and the provisions of Schedules 3 and 4 (consequential amendments and repeals) extend to Scotland so far as they relate to enactments which so extend, subject as follows.

(4) The repeal of the Arbitration Act 1975 extends only to England and Wales and Northern Ireland.

109 Commencement

(1) The provisions of this Act come into force on such day as the Secretary of State may appoint by order made by statutory instrument, and different days may be appointed for different purposes.

(2) An order under subsection (1) may contain such transitional provisions as appear to the Secretary of State to be appropriate.

110 Short title

This Act may be cited as the Arbitration Act 1996.

SCHEDULES

SCHEDULE 1

Section 4(1).

MANDATORY PROVISIONS OF PART I

sections 9 to 11 (stay of legal proceedings);
section 12 (power of court to extend agreed time limits);
section 13 (application of Limitation Acts);
section 24 (power of court to remove arbitrator);
section 26(1) (effect of death of arbitrator);
section 28 (liability of parties for fees and expenses of arbitrators);
section 29 (immunity of arbitrator);
section 31 (objection to substantive jurisdiction of tribunal);
section 32 (determination of preliminary point of jurisdiction);
section 33 (general duty of tribunal);
section 37(2) (items to be treated as expenses of arbitrators);
section 40 (general duty of parties);
section 43 (securing the attendance of witnesses);
section 56 (power to withhold award in case of non-payment);
section 60 (effectiveness of agreement for payment of costs in any event);
section 66 (enforcement of award);
sections 67 and 68 (challenging the award: substantive jurisdiction and serious irregularity), and sections 70 and 71 (supplementary provisions; effect of order of court) so far as relating to those sections;
section 72 (saving for rights of person who takes no part in proceedings);
section 73 (loss of right to object);
section 74 (immunity of arbitral institutions, &c.);
section 75 (charge to secure payment of solicitors' costs).

SCHEDULE 2

Section 93(6).

MODIFICATIONS OF PART I IN RELATION TO JUDGE-ARBITRATORS

Introductory

1 In this Schedule "judge-arbitrator" means a judge of the Commercial Court or official referee appointed as arbitrator or umpire under section 93.

General

2 (1) Subject to the following provisions of this Schedule, references in Part I to the court shall be construed in relation to a judge-arbitrator, or in relation to the appointment of a judge-arbitrator, as references to the Court of Appeal.

(2) The references in sections 32(6), 45(6) and 69(8) to the Court of Appeal shall in such a case be construed as references to the House of Lords.

Arbitrator's fees

3 (1) The power of the court in section 28(2) to order consideration and adjustment of the liability of a party for the fees of an arbitrator may be exercised by a judge-arbitrator.

(2) Any such exercise of the power is subject to the powers of the Court of Appeal under sections 24(4) and 25(3)(b) (directions as to entitlement to fees or expenses in case of removal or resignation).

Exercise of court powers in support of arbitration

4 (1) Where the arbitral tribunal consists of or includes a judge-arbitrator the powers of the court under sections 42 to 44 (enforcement of peremptory orders, summoning witnesses, and other court powers) are exercisable by the High Court and also by the judge-arbitrator himself.

(2) Anything done by a judge-arbitrator in the exercise of those powers shall be regarded as done by him in his capacity as judge of the High Court and have effect as if done by that court.

Nothing in this sub-paragraph prejudices any power vested in him as arbitrator or umpire.

Extension of time for making award

5 (1) The power conferred by section 50 (extension of time for making award) is exercisable by the judge-arbitrator himself.

(2) Any appeal from a decision of a judge-arbitrator under that section lies to the Court of Appeal with the leave of that court.

Withholding award in case of non-payment

6 (1) The provisions of paragraph 7 apply in place of the provisions of section 56 (power to withhold award in the case of non-payment) in relation to the withholding of an award for non-payment of the fees and expenses of a judge-arbitrator.

(2) This does not affect the application of section 56 in relation to the delivery of such an award by an arbitral or other institution or person vested by the parties with powers in relation to the delivery of the award.

7 (1) A judge-arbitrator may refuse to deliver an award except upon payment of the fees and expenses mentioned in section 56(1).

(2) The judge-arbitrator may, on an application by a party to the arbitral proceedings, order that if he pays into the High Court the fees and expenses demanded, or such lesser amount as the judge-arbitrator may specify—

(a) the award shall be delivered,

(b) the amount of the fees and expenses properly payable shall be determined by such means and upon such terms as he may direct, and

(c) out of the money paid into court there shall be paid out such fees and expenses as may be found to be properly payable and the balance of the money (if any) shall be paid out to the applicant.

(3) For this purpose the amount of fees and expenses properly payable is the amount the applicant is liable to pay under section 28 or any agreement relating to the payment of the arbitrator.

(4) No application to the judge-arbitrator under this paragraph may be made where there is any available arbitral process for appeal or review of the amount of the fees or expenses demanded.

(5) Any appeal from a decision of a judge-arbitrator under this paragraph lies to the Court of Appeal with the leave of that court.

(6) Where a party to arbitral proceedings appeals under sub-paragraph (5), an arbitrator is entitled to appear and be heard.

Correction of award or additional award

8 Subsections (4) to (6) of section 57 (correction of award or additional award: time limit for application or exercise of power) do not apply to a judge-arbitrator.

Costs

9 Where the arbitral tribunal consists of or includes a judge-arbitrator the powers of the court under section 63(4) (determination of recoverable costs) shall be exercised by the High Court.

10 (1) The power of the court under section 64 to determine an arbitrator's reasonable fees and expenses may be exercised by a judge-arbitrator.

(2) Any such exercise of the power is subject to the powers of the Court of Appeal under sections 24(4) and 25(3)(b) (directions as to entitlement to fees or expenses in case of removal or resignation).

Enforcement of award

11 The leave of the court required by section 66 (enforcement of award) may in the case of an award of a judge-arbitrator be given by the judge-arbitrator himself.

Solicitors' costs

12 The powers of the court to make declarations and orders under the provisions applied by section 75 (power to charge property recovered in arbitral proceedings with the payment of solicitors' costs) may be exercised by the judge-arbitrator.

Powers of court in relation to service of documents

13 (1) The power of the court under section 77(2) (powers of court in relation to service of documents) is exercisable by the judge-arbitrator.

(2) Any appeal from a decision of a judge-arbitrator under that section lies to the Court of Appeal with the leave of that court.

Powers of court to extend time limits relating to arbitral proceedings

14 (1) The power conferred by section 79 (power of court to extend time limits relating to arbitral proceedings) is exercisable by the judge-arbitrator himself.

(2) Any appeal from a decision of a judge-arbitrator under that section lies to the Court of Appeal with the leave of that court.

SCHEDULE 3

Section 107(1).

CONSEQUENTIAL AMENDMENTS

Merchant Shipping Act 1894 (c. 60)

1 In section 496 of the Merchant Shipping Act 1894 (provisions as to deposits by owners of goods), after subsection (4) insert—

"(5) In subsection (3) the expression "legal proceedings" includes arbitral proceedings and as respects England and Wales and Northern Ireland the provisions of section 14 of the Arbitration Act 1996 apply to determine when such proceedings are commenced.".

Stannaries Court (Abolition) Act 1896 (c. 45)

2 In section 4(1) of the Stannaries Court (Abolition) Act 1896 (references of certain disputes to arbitration), for the words from "tried before" to "any such reference" substitute "referred to arbitration before himself or before an arbitrator agreed on by the parties or an officer of the court".

Tithe Act 1936 (c. 43)

3 In section 39(1) of the Tithe Act 1936 (proceedings of Tithe Redemption Commission)—

(a) for "the Arbitration Acts 1889 to 1934" substitute "Part I of the Arbitration Act 1996";

(b) for paragraph (e) substitute—

"(e) the making of an application to the court to determine a preliminary point of law and the bringing of an appeal to the court on a point of law;";

(c) for "the said Acts" substitute "Part I of the Arbitration Act 1996".

Education Act 1944 (c. 31)

4 In section 75(2) of the Education Act 1944 (proceedings of Independent School Tribunals) for "the Arbitration Acts 1889 to 1934" substitute "Part I of the Arbitration Act 1996".

Commonwealth Telegraphs Act 1949 (c. 39)

5 In section 8(2) of the Commonwealth Telegraphs Act 1949 (proceedings of referees under the Act) for "the Arbitration Acts 1889 to 1934, or the Arbitration Act (Northern Ireland) 1937," substitute "Part I of the Arbitration Act 1996".

Lands Tribunal Act 1949 (c. 42)

6 In section 3 of the Lands Tribunal Act 1949 (proceedings before the Lands Tribunal) —

(a) in subsection (6)(c) (procedural rules: power to apply Arbitration Acts), and

(b) in subsection (8) (exclusion of Arbitration Acts except as applied by rules),

for "the Arbitration Acts 1889 to 1934" substitute "Part I of the Arbitration Act 1996".

Wireless Telegraphy Act 1949 (c. 54)

7 In the Wireless Telegraphy Act 1949, Schedule 2 (procedure of appeals tribunal), in paragraph 3(1)—

(a) for the words "the Arbitration Acts 1889 to 1934" substitute "Part I of the Arbitration Act 1996";

(b) after the word "Wales" insert "or Northern Ireland"; and

(c) for "the said Acts" substitute "Part I of that Act".

Patents Act 1949 (c. 87)

8 In section 67 of the Patents Act 1949 (proceedings as to infringement of pre-1978 patents referred to comptroller), for "The Arbitration Acts 1889 to 1934" substitute "Part I of the Arbitration Act 1996".

National Health Service (Amendment) Act 1949 (c. 93)

9 In section 7(8) of the National Health Service (Amendment) Act 1949 (arbitration in relation to hardship arising from the National Health Service Act 1946 or the Act), for "the Arbitration Acts 1889 to 1934" substitute "Part I of the Arbitration Act 1996" and for "the said Acts" substitute "Part I of that Act".

Arbitration Act 1950 (c. 27)

10 In section 36(1) of the Arbitration Act 1950 (effect of foreign awards enforceable under Part II of that Act) for "section 26 of this Act" substitute "section 66 of the Arbitration Act 1996".

Interpretation Act (Northern Ireland) 1954 (c. 33 (N.I.))

11 In section 46(2) of the Interpretation Act (Northern Ireland) 1954 (miscellaneous definitions), for the definition of "arbitrator" substitute—

""arbitrator" has the same meaning as in Part I of the Arbitration Act 1996;".

Agricultural Marketing Act 1958 (c. 47)

12 In section 12(1) of the Agricultural Marketing Act 1958 (application of provisions of Arbitration Act 1950)—

(a) for the words from the beginning to "shall apply" substitute "Sections 45 and 69 of the Arbitration Act 1996 (which relate to the determination by the court of questions of law) and section 66 of that Act (enforcement of awards) apply"; and

(b) for "an arbitration" substitute "arbitral proceedings".

Carriage by Air Act 1961 (c. 27)

13 (1) The Carriage by Air Act 1961 is amended as follows.

(2) In section 5(3) (time for bringing proceedings)—

(a) for "an arbitration" in the first place where it occurs substitute "arbitral proceedings"; and

(b) for the words from "and subsections (3) and (4)" to the end substitute "and the provisions of section 14 of the Arbitration Act 1996 apply to determine when such proceedings are commenced.".

(3) In section 11(c) (application of section 5 to Scotland)—

(a) for "subsections (3) and (4)" substitute "the provisions of section 14 of the Arbitration Act 1996"; and

(b) for "an arbitration" substitute "arbitral proceedings".

Factories Act 1961 (c. 34)

14 In the Factories Act 1961, for section 171 (application of Arbitration Act 1950), substitute—

"171 Application of the Arbitration Act 1996

"171 "171 Application of the Arbitration Act 1996

Part I of the Arbitration Act 1996 does not apply to proceedings under this Act except in so far as it may be applied by regulations made under this Act.".

Clergy Pensions Measure 1961 (No. 3)

15 In the Clergy Pensions Measure 1961, section 38(4) (determination of questions), for the words "The Arbitration Act 1950" substitute "Part I of the Arbitration Act 1996".

Transport Act 1962 (c. 46)

16 (1) The Transport Act 1962 is amended as follows.

(2) In section 74(6)(f) (proceedings before referees in pension disputes), for the words "the Arbitration Act 1950" substitute "Part I of the Arbitration Act 1996".

(3) In section 81(7) (proceedings before referees in compensation disputes), for the words "the Arbitration Act 1950" substitute "Part I of the Arbitration Act 1996".

(4) In Schedule 7, Part IV (pensions), in paragraph 17(5) for the words "the Arbitration Act 1950" substitute "Part I of the Arbitration Act 1996".

Corn Rents Act 1963 (c. 14)

17 In the Corn Rents Act 1963, section 1(5) (schemes for apportioning corn rents, &c.), for the words "the Arbitration Act 1950" substitute "Part I of the Arbitration Act 1996".

Plant Varieties and Seeds Act 1964 (c. 14)

18 In section 10(6) of the Plant Varieties and Seeds Act 1964 (meaning of "arbitration agreement"), for "the meaning given by section 32 of the Arbitration Act 1950" substitute "the same meaning as in Part I of the Arbitration Act 1996".

Lands Tribunal and Compensation Act (Northern Ireland) 1964 (c. 29 (N.I.))

19 In section 9 of the Lands Tribunal and Compensation Act (Northern Ireland) 1964 (proceedings of Lands Tribunal), in subsection (3) (where Tribunal acts as arbitrator) for "the Arbitration Act (Northern Ireland) 1937" substitute "Part I of the Arbitration Act 1996".

Industrial and Provident Societies Act 1965 (c. 12)

20 (1) Section 60 of the Industrial and Provident Societies Act 1965 is amended as follows.

(2) In subsection (8) (procedure for hearing disputes between society and member, &c.) —

(a) in paragraph (a) for "the Arbitration Act 1950" substitute "Part I of the Arbitration Act 1996"; and

(b) in paragraph (b) omit "by virtue of section 12 of the said Act of 1950".

(3) For subsection (9) substitute—

"(9) The court or registrar to whom any dispute is referred under subsections (2) to (7) may at the request of either party state a case on any question of law arising in the dispute for the opinion of the High Court or, as the case may be, the Court of Session.".

Carriage of Goods by Road Act 1965 (c. 37)

21 In section 7(2) of the Carriage of Goods by Road Act 1965 (arbitrations: time at which deemed to commence), for paragraphs (a) and (b) substitute—

"(a) as respects England and Wales and Northern Ireland, the provisions of section 14(3) to (5) of the Arbitration Act 1996 (which determine the time at which an arbitration is commenced) apply;".

Factories Act (Northern Ireland) 1965 (c. 20 (N.I.))

22 In section 171 of the Factories Act (Northern Ireland) 1965 (application of Arbitration Act), for "The Arbitration Act (Northern Ireland) 1937" substitute "Part I of the Arbitration Act 1996".

Commonwealth Secretariat Act 1966 (c. 10)

23 In section 1(3) of the Commonwealth Secretariat Act 1966 (contracts with Commonwealth Secretariat to be deemed to contain provision for arbitration), for "the Arbitration Act 1950 and the Arbitration Act (Northern Ireland) 1937" substitute "Part I of the Arbitration Act 1996".

Arbitration (International Investment Disputes) Act 1966 (c. 41)

24 In the Arbitration (International Investment Disputes) Act 1966, for section 3 (application of Arbitration Act 1950 and other enactments) substitute—

"3 Application of provisions of Arbitration Act 1996

"3 **"3 Application of provisions of Arbitration Act 1996**

(1) The Lord Chancellor may by order direct that any of the provisions contained in sections 36 and 38 to 44 of the Arbitration Act 1996 (provisions concerning the conduct of arbitral proceedings, &c.) shall apply to such proceedings pursuant to the Convention as are specified in the order with or without any modifications or exceptions specified in the order.

(2) Subject to subsection (1), the Arbitration Act 1996 shall not apply to proceedings pursuant to the Convention, but this subsection shall not be taken as affecting section 9 of that Act (stay of legal proceedings in respect of matter subject to arbitration).

(3) An order made under this section—

(a) may be varied or revoked by a subsequent order so made, and

(b) shall be contained in a statutory instrument.".

Poultry Improvement Act (Northern Ireland) 1968 (c. 12 (N.I.))

25 In paragraph 10(4) of the Schedule to the Poultry Improvement Act (Northern Ireland) 1968 (reference of disputes), for "The Arbitration Act (Northern Ireland) 1937" substitute "Part I of the Arbitration Act 1996".

Industrial and Provident Societies Act (Northern Ireland) 1969 (c. 24 (N.I.))

26 (1) Section 69 of the Industrial and Provident Societies Act (Northern Ireland) 1969 (decision of disputes) is amended as follows.

(2) In subsection (7) (decision of disputes)—

(a) in the opening words, omit the words from "and without prejudice" to "1937";

(b) at the beginning of paragraph (a) insert "without prejudice to any powers exercisable by virtue of Part I of the Arbitration Act 1996,"; and

(c) in paragraph (b) omit "the registrar or" and "registrar or" and for the words from "as might have been granted by the High Court" to the end substitute "as might be granted by the registrar".

(3) For subsection (8) substitute—

"(8) The court or registrar to whom any dispute is referred under subsections (2) to (6) may at the request of either party state a case on any question of law arising in the dispute for the opinion of the High Court.".

Health and Personal Social Services (Northern Ireland) Order 1972 (N.I.14)

27 In Article 105(6) of the Health and Personal Social Services (Northern Ireland) Order 1972 (arbitrations under the Order), for "the Arbitration Act (Northern Ireland) 1937" substitute "Part I of the Arbitration Act 1996".

Consumer Credit Act 1974 (c. 39)

28 (1) Section 146 of the Consumer Credit Act 1974 is amended as follows.

(2) In subsection (2) (solicitor engaged in contentious business), for "section 86(1) of the Solicitors Act 1957" substitute "section 87(1) of the Solicitors Act 1974".

(3) In subsection (4) (solicitor in Northern Ireland engaged in contentious business), for the words from "business done" to "Administration of Estates (Northern Ireland) Order 1979" substitute "contentious business (as defined in Article 3(2) of the Solicitors (Northern Ireland) Order 1976.".

Friendly Societies Act 1974 (c. 46)

29 (1) The Friendly Societies Act 1974 is amended as follows.

(2) For section 78(1) (statement of case) substitute—

"(1) Any arbitrator, arbiter or umpire to whom a dispute falling within section 76 above is referred under the rules of a registered society or branch may at the request of either party state a case on any question of law arising in the dispute for the opinion of the High Court or, as the case may be, the Court of Session.".

(3) In section 83(3) (procedure on objections to amalgamations &c. of friendly societies), for "the Arbitration Act 1950 or, in Northern Ireland, the Arbitration Act (Northern Ireland) 1937" substitute "Part I of the Arbitration Act 1996".

Industry Act 1975 (c. 68)

30 In Schedule 3 to the Industry Act (arbitration of disputes relating to vesting and compensation orders), in paragraph 14 (application of certain provisions of Arbitration Acts)—

(a) for "the Arbitration Act 1950 or, in Northern Ireland, the Arbitration Act (Northern Ireland) 1937" substitute "Part I of the Arbitration Act 1996", and

(b) for "that Act" substitute "that Part".

Industrial Relations (Northern Ireland) Order 1976 (N.I.16)

31 In Article 59(9) of the Industrial Relations (Northern Ireland) Order 1976 (proceedings of industrial tribunal), for "The Arbitration Act (Northern Ireland) 1937" substitute "Part I of the Arbitration Act 1996".

Aircraft and Shipbuilding Industries Act 1977 (c. 3)

32 In Schedule 7 to the Aircraft and Shipbuilding Industries Act 1977 (procedure of Arbitration Tribunal), in paragraph 2—

(a) for "the Arbitration Act 1950 or, in Northern Ireland, the Arbitration Act (Northern Ireland) 1937" substitute "Part I of the Arbitration Act 1996", and

(b) for "that Act" substitute "that Part".

Patents Act 1977 (c. 37)

33 In section 130 of the Patents Act 1977 (interpretation), in subsection (8) (exclusion of Arbitration Act) for "The Arbitration Act 1950" substitute "Part I of the Arbitration Act 1996".

Judicature (Northern Ireland) Act 1978 (c. 23)

34 (1) The Judicature (Northern Ireland) Act 1978 is amended as follows.

(2) In section 35(2) (restrictions on appeals to the Court of Appeal), after paragraph (f) insert—

"(fa) except as provided by Part I of the Arbitration Act 1996, from any decision of the High Court under that Part;".

(3) In section 55(2) (rules of court) after paragraph (c) insert—

"(cc) providing for any prescribed part of the jurisdiction of the High Court in relation to the trial of any action involving matters of account to be exercised in the prescribed manner by a person agreed by the parties and for the remuneration of any such person;".

Health and Safety at Work (Northern Ireland) Order 1978 (N.I.9)

35 In Schedule 4 to the Health and Safety at Work (Northern Ireland) Order 1978 (licensing provisions), in paragraph 3, for "The Arbitration Act (Northern Ireland) 1937" substitute "Part I of the Arbitration Act 1996".

County Courts (Northern Ireland) Order 1980 (N.I.3)

36 (1) The County Courts (Northern Ireland) Order 1980 is amended as follows.

(2) In Article 30 (civil jurisdiction exercisable by district judge)—

(a) for paragraph (2) substitute—

"(2) Any order, decision or determination made by a district judge under this Article (other than one made in dealing with a claim by way of arbitration under paragraph (3)) shall be embodied in a decree which for all purposes (including the right of appeal under Part VI) shall have the like effect as a decree pronounced by a county court judge.";

(b) for paragraphs (4) and (5) substitute—

"(4) Where in any action to which paragraph (1) applies the claim is dealt with by way of arbitration under paragraph (3)—

(a) any award made by the district judge in dealing with the claim shall be embodied in a decree which for all purposes (except the right of appeal under Part VI) shall have the like effect as a decree pronounced by a county court judge;

(b) the district judge may, and shall if so required by the High Court, state for the determination of the High Court any question of law arising out of an award so made;

(c) except as provided by sub-paragraph (b), any award so made shall be final; and

(d) except as otherwise provided by county court rules, no costs shall be awarded in connection with the action.

(5) Subject to paragraph (4), county court rules may—

(a) apply any of the provisions of Part I of the Arbitration Act 1996 to arbitrations under paragraph (3) with such modifications as may be prescribed;

(b) prescribe the rules of evidence to be followed on any arbitration under paragraph (3) and, in particular, make provision with respect to the manner of taking and questioning evidence.

(5A) Except as provided by virtue of paragraph (5)(a), Part I of the Arbitration Act 1996 shall not apply to an arbitration under paragraph (3).".

(3) After Article 61 insert—

"Appeals from decisions under Part I of Arbitration Act 1996

61A(1) Article 61 does not apply to a decision of a county court judge made in the exercise of the jurisdiction conferred by Part I of the Arbitration Act 1996.

(2) Any party dissatisfied with a decision of the county court made in the exercise of the jurisdiction conferred by any of the following provisions of Part I of the Arbitration Act 1996, namely—

(a) section 32 (question as to substantive jurisdiction of arbitral tribunal);

(b) section 45 (question of law arising in course of arbitral proceedings);

(c) section 67 (challenging award of arbitral tribunal: substantive jurisdiction);

(d) section 68 (challenging award of arbitral tribunal: serious irregularity);

(e) section 69 (appeal on point of law),

may, subject to the provisions of that Part, appeal from that decision to the Court of Appeal.

(3) Any party dissatisfied with any decision of a county court made in the exercise of the jurisdiction conferred by any other provision of Part I of the Arbitration Act 1996 may, subject to the provisions of that Part, appeal from that decision to the High Court.

(4) The decision of the Court of Appeal on an appeal under paragraph (2) shall be final.".

Supreme Court Act 1981 (c. 54)

37 (1) The Supreme Court Act 1981 is amended as follows.

(2) In section 18(1) (restrictions on appeals to the Court of Appeal), for paragraph (g) substitute—

"(g) except as provided by Part I of the Arbitration Act 1996, from any decision of the High Court under that Part;".

(3) In section 151 (interpretation, &c.), in the definition of "arbitration agreement", for "the Arbitration Act 1950 by virtue of section 32 of that Act;" substitute "Part I of the Arbitration Act 1996;".

Merchant Shipping (Liner Conferences) Act 1982 (c. 37)

38 In section 7(5) of the Merchant Shipping (Liner Conferences) Act 1982 (stay of legal proceedings), for the words from "section 4(1)" to the end substitute "section 9 of the Arbitration Act 1996 (which also provides for the staying of legal proceedings).".

Agricultural Marketing (Northern Ireland) Order 1982 (N.I.12)

39 In Article 14 of the Agricultural Marketing (Northern Ireland) Order 1982 (application of provisions of Arbitration Act (Northern Ireland) 1937)—

(a) for the words from the beginning to "shall apply" substitute "Section 45 and 69 of the Arbitration Act 1996 (which relate to the determination by the court of questions of law) and section 66 of that Act (enforcement of awards)" apply; and

(b) for "an arbitration" substitute "arbitral proceedings".

Mental Health Act 1983 (c. 20)

40 In section 78 of the Mental Health Act 1983 (procedure of Mental Health Review Tribunals), in subsection (9) for "The Arbitration Act 1950" substitute "Part I of the Arbitration Act 1996".

Registered Homes Act 1984 (c. 23)

41 In section 43 of the Registered Homes Act 1984 (procedure of Registered Homes Tribunals), in subsection (3) for "The Arbitration Act 1950" substitute "Part I of the Arbitration Act 1996".

Housing Act 1985 (c. 68)

42 In section 47(3) of the Housing Act 1985 (agreement as to determination of matters relating to service charges) for "section 32 of the Arbitration Act 1950" substitute "Part I of the Arbitration Act 1996".

Landlord and Tenant Act 1985 (c. 70)

43 In section 19(3) of the Landlord and Tenant Act 1985 (agreement as to determination of matters relating to service charges), for "section 32 of the Arbitration Act 1950" substitute "Part I of the Arbitration Act 1996".

Credit Unions (Northern Ireland) Order 1985 (N.I.12)

44 (1) Article 72 of the Credit Unions (Northern Ireland) Order 1985 (decision of disputes) is amended as follows.

(2) In paragraph (7)—

(a) in the opening words, omit the words from "and without prejudice" to "1937";

(b) at the beginning of sub-paragraph (a) insert "without prejudice to any powers exercisable by virtue of Part I of the Arbitration Act 1996,"; and

(c) in sub-paragraph (b) omit "the registrar or" and "registrar or" and for the words from "as might have been granted by the High Court" to the end substitute "as might be granted by the registrar".

(3) For paragraph (8) substitute—

"(8) The court or registrar to whom any dispute is referred under paragraphs (2) to (6) may at the request of either party state a case on any question of law arising in the dispute for the opinion of the High Court.".

Agricultural Holdings Act 1986 (c. 5)

45 In section 84(1) of the Agricultural Holdings Act 1986 (provisions relating to arbitration), for "the Arbitration Act 1950" substitute "Part I of the Arbitration Act 1996".

Insolvency Act 1986 (c. 45)

46 In the Insolvency Act 1986, after section 349 insert—

"349A Arbitration agreements to which bankrupt is party

"349A "349A Arbitration agreements to which bankrupt is party

(1) This section applies where a bankrupt had become party to a contract containing an arbitration agreement before the commencement of his bankruptcy.

(2) If the trustee in bankruptcy adopts the contract, the arbitration agreement is enforceable by or against the trustee in relation to matters arising from or connected with the contract.

(3) If the trustee in bankruptcy does not adopt the contract and a matter to which the arbitration agreement applies requires to be determined in connection with or for the purposes of the bankruptcy proceedings—

(a) the trustee with the consent of the creditors' committee, or

(b) any other party to the agreement,

may apply to the court which may, if it thinks fit in all the circumstances of the case, order that the matter be referred to arbitration in accordance with the arbitration agreement.

(4) In this section—

"arbitration agreement" has the same meaning as in Part I of the Arbitration Act 1996; and "the court" means the court which has jurisdiction in the bankruptcy proceedings.".

Building Societies Act 1986 (c. 53)

47 In Part II of Schedule 14 to the Building Societies Act 1986 (settlement of disputes: arbitration), in paragraph 5(6) for "the Arbitration Act 1950 and the Arbitration Act 1979 or, in Northern Ireland, the Arbitration Act (Northern Ireland) 1937" substitute "Part I of the Arbitration Act 1996".

Mental Health (Northern Ireland) Order 1986 (N.I.4)

48 In Article 83 of the Mental Health (Northern Ireland) Order 1986 (procedure of Mental Health Review Tribunal), in paragraph (8) for "The Arbitration Act (Northern Ireland) 1937" substitute "Part I of the Arbitration Act 1996".

Multilateral Investment Guarantee Agency Act 1988 (c. 8)

49 For section 6 of the Multilateral Investment Guarantee Agency Act 1988 (application of Arbitration Act) substitute—

"6 Application of Arbitration Act

"6 "6 Application of Arbitration Act

(1) The Lord Chancellor may by order made by statutory instrument direct that any of the provisions of sections 36 and 38 to 44 of the Arbitration Act 1996 (provisions in relation to the conduct of the arbitral proceedings, &c.) apply, with such modifications or exceptions as are specified in the order, to such arbitration proceedings pursuant to Annex II to the Convention as are specified in the order.

(2) Except as provided by an order under subsection (1) above, no provision of Part I of the Arbitration Act 1996 other than section 9 (stay of legal proceedings) applies to any such proceedings.".

Copyright, Designs and Patents Act 1988 (c. 48)

50 In section 150 of the Copyright, Designs and Patents Act 1988 (Lord Chancellor's power to make rules for Copyright Tribunal), for subsection (2) substitute—

"(2) The rules may apply in relation to the Tribunal, as respects proceedings in England and Wales or Northern Ireland, any of the provisions of Part I of the Arbitration Act 1996.".

Fair Employment (Northern Ireland) Act 1989 (c. 32)

51 In the Fair Employment (Northern Ireland) Act 1989, section 5(7) (procedure of Fair Employment Tribunal), for "The Arbitration Act (Northern Ireland) 1937" substitute "Part I of the Arbitration Act 1996".

Limitation (Northern Ireland) Order 1989 (N.I.11)

52 In Article 2(2) of the Limitation (Northern Ireland) Order 1989 (interpretation), in the definition of "arbitration agreement", for "the Arbitration Act (Northern Ireland) 1937" substitute "Part I of the Arbitration Act 1996".

Insolvency (Northern Ireland) Order 1989 (N.I.19)

53 In the Insolvency (Northern Ireland) Order 1989, after Article 320 insert—

"Arbitration agreements to which bankrupt is party.

320A(1) This Article applies where a bankrupt had become party to a contract containing an arbitration agreement before the commencement of his bankruptcy.

(2) If the trustee in bankruptcy adopts the contract, the arbitration agreement is enforceable by or against the trustee in relation to matters arising from or connected with the contract.

(3) If the trustee in bankruptcy does not adopt the contract and a matter to which the arbitration agreement applies requires to be determined in connection with or for the purposes of the bankruptcy proceedings—

(a) the trustee with the consent of the creditors' committee, or

(b) any other party to the agreement,

may apply to the court which may, if it thinks fit in all the circumstances of the case, order that the matter be referred to arbitration in accordance with the arbitration agreement.

(4) In this Article—

"arbitration agreement" has the same meaning as in Part I of the Arbitration Act 1996; and

"the court" means the court which has jurisdiction in the bankruptcy proceedings.".

Social Security Administration Act 1992 (c. 5)

54 In section 59 of the Social Security Administration Act 1992 (procedure for inquiries, &c.), in subsection (7), for "The Arbitration Act 1950" substitute "Part I of the Arbitration Act 1996".

Social Security Administration (Northern Ireland) Act 1992 (c. 8)

55 In section 57 of the Social Security Administration (Northern Ireland) Act 1992 (procedure for inquiries, &c.), in subsection (6) for "the Arbitration Act (Northern Ireland) 1937" substitute "Part I of the Arbitration Act 1996".

Trade Union and Labour Relations (Consolidation) Act 1992 (c. 52)

56 In sections 212(5) and 263(6) of the Trade Union and Labour Relations (Consolidation) Act 1992 (application of Arbitration Act) for "the Arbitration Act 1950" substitute "Part I of the Arbitration Act 1996".

Industrial Relations (Northern Ireland) Order 1992 (N.I.5)

57 In Articles 84(9) and 92(5) of the Industrial Relations (Northern Ireland) Order 1992 (application of Arbitration Act) for "The Arbitration Act (Northern Ireland) 1937" substitute "Part I of the Arbitration Act 1996".

Registered Homes (Northern Ireland) Order 1992 (N.I.20)

58 In Article 33(3) of the Registered Homes (Northern Ireland) Order 1992 (procedure of Registered Homes Tribunal) for "The Arbitration Act (Northern Ireland) 1937" substitute "Part I of the Arbitration Act 1996".

Education Act 1993 (c. 35)

59 In section 180(4) of the Education Act 1993 (procedure of Special Educational Needs Tribunal), for "The Arbitration Act 1950" substitute "Part I of the Arbitration Act 1996".

Roads (Northern Ireland) Order 1993 (N.I.15)

60 (1) The Roads (Northern Ireland) Order 1993 is amended as follows.

(2) In Article 131 (application of Arbitration Act) for "the Arbitration Act (Northern Ireland) 1937" substitute "Part I of the Arbitration Act 1996".

(3) In Schedule 4 (disputes), in paragraph 3(2) for "the Arbitration Act (Northern Ireland) 1937" substitute "Part I of the Arbitration Act 1996".

Merchant Shipping Act 1995 (c. 21)

61 In Part II of Schedule 6 to the Merchant Shipping Act 1995 (provisions having effect in connection with Convention Relating to the Carriage of Passengers and Their Luggage by Sea), for paragraph 7 substitute—

"7 Article 16 shall apply to arbitral proceedings as it applies to an action; and, as respects England and Wales and Northern Ireland, the provisions of section 14 of the Arbitration Act 1996 apply to determine for the purposes of that Article when an arbitration is commenced.".

Industrial Tribunals Act 1996 (c. 17)

62 In section 6(2) of the Industrial Tribunals Act 1996 (procedure of industrial tribunals), for "The Arbitration Act 1950" substitute "Part I of the Arbitration Act 1996".

SCHEDULE 4

Section 107(2).

REPEALS

Chapter	*Short title*	*Extent of repeal*
1892 c. 43.	Military Lands Act 1892.	In section 21(b), the words "under the Arbitration Act 1889".
1922 c. 51.	Allotments Act 1922.	In section 21(3), the words "under the Arbitration Act 1889".
1937 c. 8 (N.I.).	Arbitration Act (Northern Ireland) 1937.	The whole Act.
1949 c. 54.	Wireless Telegraphy Act 1949.	In Schedule 2, paragraph 3(3).
1949 c. 97.	National Parks and Access to the Countryside Act 1949.	In section 18(4), the words from "Without prejudice" to "England or Wales".
1950 c. 27.	Arbitration Act 1950.	Part I. Section 42(3).
1958 c. 47.	Agricultural Marketing Act 1958.	Section 53(8).
1962 c. 46.	Transport Act 1962.	In Schedule 11, Part II, paragraph 7.
1964 c. 14.	Plant Varieties and Seeds Act 1964.	In section 10(4) the words from "or in section 9" to "three arbitrators)". Section 39(3)(b)(i).
1964 c. 29 (N.I.).	Lands Tribunal and Compensation Act (Northern Ireland) 1964.	In section 9(3) the words from "so, however, that" to the end.
1965 c. 12.	Industrial and Provident Societies Act 1965.	In section 60(8)(b), the words "by virtue of section 12 of the said Act of 1950".
1965 c. 37.	Carriage of Goods by Road Act 1965.	Section 7(2)(b).
1965 c. 13 (N.I.).	New Towns Act (Northern Ireland) 1965.	In section 27(2), the words from "under and in accordance with" to the end.
1969 c. 24 (N.I.).	Industrial and Provident Societies Act (Northern Ireland) 1969.	In section 69(7)— (a) in the opening words, the words from "and without prejudice" to "1937";

Chapter	*Short title*	*Extent of repeal*
		(b) in paragraph (b), the words "the registrar or" and "registrar or".
1970 c. 31.	Administration of Justice Act 1970.	Section 4. Schedule 3.
1973 c. 41.	Fair Trading Act 1973.	Section 33(2)(d).
1973 N.I. 1.	Drainage (Northern Ireland) Order 1973.	In Article 15(4), the words from "under and in accordance" to the end. Article 40(4). In Schedule 7, in paragraph 9(2), the words from "under and in accordance" to the end.
1974 c. 47.	Solicitors Act 1974.	In section 87(1), in the definition of "contentious business", the words "appointed under the Arbitration Act 1950".
1975 c. 3.	Arbitration Act 1975.	The whole Act.
1975 c. 74. In Part II of Schedule 3, in model clause 38(2), the words "in accordance with the Arbitration Act 1950".	Petroleum and Submarine Pipe-Lines Act 1975.	In Part II of Schedule 2— (a) in model clause 40(2), the words "in accordance with the Arbitration Act 1950"; (b) in model clause 40(2B), the words "in accordance with the Arbitration Act (Northern Ireland) 1937".
1976 N.I. 12.	Solicitors (Northern Ireland) Order 1976.	In Article 3(2), in the entry "contentious business", the words "appointed under the Arbitration Act (Northern Ireland) 1937". Article 71H(3).
1977 c. 37.	Patents Act 1977.	In section 52(4) the words "section 21 of the Arbitration Act 1950 or, as the case may be, section 22 of the Arbitration Act (Northern Ireland) 1937 (statement of cases by arbitrators); but". Section 131(e).

Chapter	*Short title*	*Extent of repeal*
1977 c. 38.	Administration of Justice Act 1977.	Section 17(2).
1978 c. 23.	Judicature (Northern Ireland) Act 1978.	In section 35(2), paragraph (g)(v). In Schedule 5, the amendment to the Arbitration Act 1950.
1979 c. 42.	Arbitration Act 1979.	The whole Act.
1980 c. 58.	Limitation Act 1980.	Section 34.
1980 N.I. 3.	County Courts (Northern Ireland) Order 1980.	Article 31(3).
1981 c. 54.	Supreme Court Act 1981.	Section 148.
1982 c. 27.	Civil Jurisdiction and Judgments Act 1982.	Section 25(3)(c) and (5). In section 26— (a) in subsection (1), the words "to arbitration or"; (b) in subsection (1)(a)(i), the words "arbitration or"; (c) in subsection (2), the words "arbitration or".
1982 c. 53.	Administration of Justice Act 1982.	Section 15(6). In Schedule 1, Part IV.
1984 c. 5.	Merchant Shipping Act 1984.	Section 4(8).
1984 c. 12.	Telecommunications Act 1984.	Schedule 2, paragraph 13(8).
1984 c. 16.	Foreign Limitation Periods Act 1984.	Section 5.
1984 c. 28.	County Courts Act 1984.	In Schedule 2, paragraph 70.
1985 c. 61.	Administration of Justice Act 1985.	Section 58. In Schedule 9, paragraph 15.
1985 c. 68.	Housing Act 1985.	In Schedule 18, in paragraph 6(2) the words from "and the Arbitration Act 1950" to the end.
1985 N.I. 12.	Credit Unions (Northern Ireland) Order 1985.	In Article 72(7)— (a) in the opening words, the words from "and without prejudice" to "1937";

Chapter	*Short title*	*Extent of repeal*
		(b) in sub-paragraph (b), the words "the registrar or" and "registrar or".
1986 c. 45.	Insolvency Act 1986.	In Schedule 14, the entry relating to the Arbitration Act 1950.
1988 c. 8.	Multilateral Investment Guarantee Agency Act 1988.	Section 8(3).
1988 c. 21.	Consumer Arbitration Agreements Act 1988.	The whole Act.
1989 N.I. 11.	Limitation (Northern Ireland) Order 1989.	Article 72.
		In Schedule 3, paragraph 1.
1989 N.I. 19.	Insolvency (Northern Ireland) Order 1989.	In Part II of Schedule 9, paragraph 66.
1990 c. 41.	Courts and Legal Services Act 1990.	Sections 99 and 101 to 103.
1991 N.I. 7.	Food Safety (Northern Ireland) Order 1991.	In Articles 8(8) and 11(10), the words from "and the provisions" to the end.
1992 c. 40.	Friendly Societies Act 1992.	In Schedule 16, paragraph 30(1).
1995 c. 8.	Agricultural Tenancies Act 1995.	Section 28(4).
1995 c. 21.	Merchant Shipping Act 1995.	Section 96(10).
		Section 264(9).
1995 c. 42.	Private International Law (Miscellaneous Provisions) Act 1995.	Section 3.

Adapted and published by GRANGIS under the OGL Licence 3.0.

www.nationalarchives.gov.uk/doc/open-government-licence/version/3/

GRANGIS - UK PUBLISHING 2022.

Thank you for taking the time to leave us a review regarding this version

★★★★★

For further inquiries, contact us at:
www.grangis.com / contact@grangis.com

www.ingramcontent.com/pod-product-compliance
Lightning Source LLC
LaVergne TN
LVHW060213210926
848481LV00008B/2732
* 9 7 9 8 8 8 5 5 9 0 0 5 1 *

GRAN*GIS* UK Publishing

Adapted and published by GRANGIS (Grand Register Library).
Online: www.grangis.com
E-mail: contact@grangis.com

In this version:
ISBN: 979-8-88559-037-2

Note: This is the original version (as it was originally enacted). Title, sub-title and the generated date is as marked on the pages.

These notes refer to the Licensing Act 2003 (c.17)

EXPLANATORY NOTES

LICENSING ACT 2003

Section 17 - Application for a premises licence

Section 18 – Determination of application for premises licence

Section 19 - Mandatory conditions where licence authorises supply of alcohol

Section 20 – Mandatory condition: exhibition of films

Section 21 – Mandatory condition: door supervision

Section 22 – Prohibited conditions: plays

Section 23 – Grant or rejection of application

Section 24 – Form of licence and summary

Section 25 - Theft, loss, of premises licence or summary

Section 26 – Period of validity of premises licence

Section 27 – Death, incapacity, insolvency of licence holder

Section 28 – Surrender of premises licence

Section 29 – Application for a provisional statement where premises being built,

Section 30 – Advertisement of application for provisional statement

Section 31 – Determination of application for provisional statement

Section 32 – Restriction on making representations following provisional statement

Section 33 – Notification of change of name or address.

Section 34 - Application to vary premises licence

Section 35 - Determination of application under section 34 and

Section 36 - Supplementary provision about determinations under section 35

Section 37 – Application to vary licence to specify individual as premises supervisor

Section 38 – Circumstances in which section 37 application given interim effect

Section 39 – Determination of section 37 application

Section 40 – Duty of applicant following determination under section 39

Section 41 – Request to be removed as designated premises supervisor

Section 42 – Application for transfer of premises licence

Section 43 – Circumstances in which transfer application given interim effect

Section 44 – Determination of transfer application

Section 72 – Determination of application for club premises certificate

Section 73 – Certificate authorising supply of alcohol for consumption off the premises

Section 74 – Mandatory condition: exhibition of films

Section 75– Prohibited conditions: associate members and their guests

Section 76– Prohibited conditions: plays

Section 77 – Grant or rejection of application for club premises certificate

Section 78 - Form of certificate and summary

Section 79 – Theft, loss of certificate or summary

Section 80 – Period of validity of club premises certificate

Section 81 - Surrender of club premises certificate

Section 82 – Notification of change of name or alteration of rules of club

Section 83 – Change of relevant registered address of a club

Section 84 – Application to vary club premises certificate

Section 85 – Determination of application under section 84 and

Section 86 – Supplementary provision about applications under section 84

Section 87 – Application for review of club premises certificate

Section88 – Determination of application for review and

Section 89 – Supplementary provision about review

Section 90 – Club ceasing to be a qualifying club

Section 91 – Form etc. of applications and notices under Part 4

Section 92 – Fees

Section 93 – Duty to provide licensing authority with club premises certificate

Section 94 - Duty to keep and produce certificate

Section 95 - Provision supplementary to section 94

Section 96 - Inspection of premises before grant of certificate

Section 97 - Other powers of entry and search

Section 98 – Meaning of 'permitted temporary activity'

Section 99– The relevant licensing authority

Section 100 – Temporary event notice

Section 101 – Minimum of 24 hours between event periods

Section 102 – Acknowledgement of notice

Section 103– Withdrawal of notice

Section 104 – Objection to notice by police

Section 105 - Counter notice following police objection and

Section 106 - Modification of notice following police objection

Section 107 - Counter notice where permitted limits exceeded

Section 108 – Right of entry where temporary event notice given and

Section 109 – Duty to keep and produce temporary event notice

Section 110 – Theft, loss of temporary event notice

Section 111 – Personal licence

Section 112 – The relevant licensing authority

Section 113 – Meaning of "relevant offence" and "foreign offence"

Section 114 – Spent convictions

Section 115 – Period of validity of personal licence and

Section 116 – Surrender of personal licence

Section 117 – Application for grant or renewal of personal licence

Section 118 – Individual permitted to hold only one personal licence

Section 119 – Licence continued pending renewal

Section 120 – Determination of application for grant

Section 121 – Determination of application for renewal

Section 122 – Notification of determinations

Section 123 – Duty to notify licensing authority of convictions during application period

Section 124 – Convictions coming to light after grant or renewal

Section 125 – Form of personal licence

Section 126 – Theft, loss, of personal licence

Section 127 – Duty to notify change of name or address

Section 128 – Duty to notify court of personal licence

Section 129 – Forfeiture or suspension of licence on conviction for relevant offence

Section 130 – Powers of appellate court to suspend order under section 129

Section 131 – Court's duty to notify licensing authority of convictions

Section 132 – Licence holder's duty to notify licensing authority of convictions

Section 133 –Form etc. of applications and notices under Part 6

Section 134 – Licensing authority's duty to update licence document

Section 135 – Licence holder's duty to produce licence

Section 136 – Unauthorised licensable activities

Section 137 – Exposing alcohol for unauthorised sale

Section 138 – Keeping alcohol on premises for unauthorised sale

Section 139 - Defence of due diligence

Section 140 – Allowing disorderly conduct on licensed premises

Section 141 – Sale of alcohol to a person who is drunk

Section 142 – Obtaining alcohol for a person who is drunk

Section 143– Failure to leave licensed premises

Section 144 – Keeping of smuggled goods

Section 145 – Unaccompanied children prohibited from certain premises.

Section 146 – Sale of alcohol to children

Section 147 – Allowing sale of alcohol to children

Section 148 – Sale of liqueur confectionery to children under 16

Section 149 – Purchase of alcohol by or on behalf of children

Section 150 – Consumption of alcohol by children

Section 151 – Delivering alcohol to children

Section 152 – Sending a child to obtain alcohol

Section 153 – Prohibition of unsupervised sales by children

Section 154 – Enforcement role for weights and measures authorities

Section 155 – Confiscation of sealed containers for alcohol

Section 156 – Prohibition of sale of alcohol on moving vehicles

Section 157 – Power to prohibit sale of alcohol on trains

These notes refer to the Licensing Act 2003 (c.17) which received Royal Assent on 10 July 2003

LICENSING ACT 2003

EXPLANATORY NOTES

INTRODUCTION

1. These explanatory notes relate to the Licensing Act 2003. They have been prepared by the Department for Culture, Media and Sport in order to assist the reader of the Act. They do not form part of the Act and have not been endorsed by Parliament.

2. The notes need to be read in conjunction with the Act. They are not, and are not meant to be, a comprehensive description of the Act. So where a section or Schedule or part of a section or Schedule does not seem to require any explanation or comment, none is given.

SUMMARY AND BACKGROUND

3. In April 2000 the Government published a White Paper on reforming alcohol and entertainment licensing (Time for Reform: Proposals for the Modernisation of Our Licensing Laws; CM 4696). This White Paper set out proposals for modernising and integrating the alcohol, public entertainment, theatre, cinema, night café and late night refreshment house licensing schemes in England and Wales. The White Paper outlined the key aims of the proposals:

    a) to reduce crime and disorder;

    b) to encourage tourism;

    c) to reduce alcohol misuse; and

    d) to encourage self-sufficient rural communities.

4. The White Paper also set out proposals for reducing the burden of unnecessary regulation. Its proposals were intended to ensure that the provision of additional opportunities for licensable activities were matched by additional measures enabling the police and licensing authorities to act promptly to maintain public order and safety.

5. Since the publication of the White Paper in 2000, responsibility for alcohol and entertainment licensing policy has been transferred from the Home Office to the Department for Culture, Media and Sport.

6. The Act provides for a unified system of regulation of the activities of the sale and supply of alcohol, the provision of regulated entertainment (see Schedule 1), and the provision of late night refreshment (see Schedule 2). In the Act, these activities are referred to collectively as "the licensable activities".

7. The purpose of the system of licensing for licensable activities is to promote four fundamental objectives ("the licensing objectives"). Those objectives are –

    a) the prevention of crime and disorder;

    b) public safety;

    c) the prevention of public nuisance; and

d) the protection of children from harm.

8. The system of licensing is achieved through the provision of authorisations through personal licences, premises licences, club premises certificates and temporary event notices.

9. Personal licences authorise individuals to sell or supply alcohol, or authorise the sale or supply of alcohol, for consumption on or off premises for which a premises licence is in force for the carrying on of that activity (see paragraph 10). To qualify for a personal licence an individual must be aged 18 or over, possess a recognised qualification and be in a position to show the licensing authority (see paragraph 34 below) that he has not been convicted of certain offences ("relevant offences" and "foreign offences", see paragraph 189 below). If a person has been convicted of a relevant offence or foreign offence, following notification to the chief officer of police and consideration of any objections from the police, the licensing authority must grant a personal licence unless it considers that doing so would undermine the crime prevention objective (see paragraph 7a) above). Personal licences last for ten years and are be renewable.

10. A premises licence authorises the holder of the licence to use the premises to which the licence relates ("the licensed premises") for licensable activities. The premises licence details operating conditions. The purpose of these conditions is to regulate the use of the premises for licensable activities in line with the licensing objectives. A premises licence has effect until the licence is revoked or surrendered, but otherwise is not time limited unless the applicant requests a licence for a limited period. Representations may be made about an application for the grant of a premises licence; for example by local residents and businesses, the police, the fire authority and public bodies with responsibility for environmental health. The representations must concern the promotion of the licensing objectives. Once the licence has been granted the same classes of persons and bodies may seek a review of the premises licence and the conditions attaching to it.

11. Club premises certificates provide authorisation for qualifying clubs (see paragraph 119 below) to use club premises for qualifying club activities. The qualifying club activities are a subset of the licensable activities. They are the supply of alcohol by or on behalf of a club to a member of the club, the sale by retail of alcohol by or on behalf of a club to a guest of a member for consumption on the premises and the provision of regulated entertainment by or on behalf of a club for its members and guests. As with premises licences, the right to make representations on the application for a club premises certificate is given to a range of persons and bodies.

12. In contrast to the existing law, the Act does not prescribe the days or the opening hours when alcohol may be sold by retail for consumption on or off premises. Nor does it specify when other licensable activities may be carried on. Instead, the applicant for a premises licence or a club premises certificate will be able to choose the days and the hours during which they wish to be authorised to carry on licensable activities at the premises for which a licence is sought. The licence will be granted on those terms unless, following the making of representations to the licensing authority, the authority considers it necessary to reject the application or vary those terms for the purpose of promoting the licensing objectives.

13. Personal licences, premises licences and club premises certificates are granted by licensing authorities under the Act, which generally will be the local authority for the area in which the premises are situated or, in the case of personal licences, in which the individual applicant is normally resident.

14. The Act provides procedures for regulating the discharge by the licensing authority of its functions. Authorities are required to publish a policy framework document every three years. In producing the document a licensing authority is required to take account of the views of those representing the holders of licences and certificates, local residents

and businesses, the police, and the fire authority. Licensing authorities are also required to take into account guidance issued by the Secretary of State.

15. In addition, the Act establishes new arrangements for the carrying on of licensable activities at occasional, temporary events. These arrangements replace systems of "occasional permissions" and "occasional licences". They apply in relation to events with less than 500 people attending. The new arrangements are based on a notification to the licensing authority of salient details of the event and an acknowledgement by that authority of the notification. To reflect the temporary nature of the events, these arrangements do not place organisers under the same obligations as apply in relation to those who regularly wish to undertake licensable activities on or from premises.

16. The Act provides for the setting of fees in relation to applications, notifications, licences and certificates. The fees will be set centrally and are intended to be set on the basis of full cost recovery. The Act requires each licensing authority to establish a register relating to the grant of licences and certificates and the giving of temporary event notices and associated matters. The Act includes a power for the Secretary of State to provide for the establishment of a central database to maintain matters a licensing authority is obliged to register.

17. The Act provides licensing authorities with the power, on review of a premises licence, to suspend or revoke the licence, to exclude specific licensable activities from the licence, or to modify operating conditions attaching to the licence. These powers must be exercised with a view to promoting the licensing objectives. These same powers attach to club premises certificates.

18. In addition, the Act confers powers on the police to close licensed premises to deal expeditiously with disorderly behaviour and excessive noise; these powers are both anticipatory and reactive.

19. The new regime will be supported by a range of offences, inspection powers and enforcement provisions.

THE ACT

20. The Act has nine parts, as follows: -

- Part 1 – licensable activities
- Part 2 – licensing authorities
- Part 3 – premises licences
- Part 4 – clubs
- Part 5 – permitted temporary activities
- Part 6 – personal licences
- Part 7 – offences
- Part 8 – closure of premises
- Part 9 – miscellaneous and supplementary

21. The Act repeals and replaces the existing licensing provisions in respect of alcohol sales and supplies, public entertainment and late night refreshment, regulated principally by the following statutes:

- London Government Act 1963, Schedule 12
- Licensing Act 1964
- Greater London Council (General Powers) Act 1966, Part IV

- Private Places of Entertainment (Licensing) Act 1967
- Theatres Act 1968
- Late Night Refreshment Houses Act 1969
- Local Government (Miscellaneous Provisions) Act 1982, Schedule 1
- Licensing (Occasional Permissions) Act 1983
- Cinemas Act 1985 and
- London Local Authorities Act 1990

22. The theatres with letters patent from the Crown, which were exempted from the requirement for a licence under the Theatres Act 1968, are brought within the licensing regime. The privileges and exemptions enjoyed by the University of Cambridge and the Vintners of the City of London in relation to the licensing of alcohol sales are not preserved by the Act.

23. The Act repeals the statutory provisions which provide that premises in Wales licensed for the sale of alcohol may open on Sundays only where there has been a vote in favour of such opening in the local government area where the premises are situated (see sections 66 and 67 of the Licensing Act 1964).

COMMENTARY ON SECTIONS

PART 1 – Licensable activities

General

24. This Part describes those activities that are covered by the Act and as a consequence prescribes those matters which are regulated by the provisions in the Act, thereby determining its scope of application. The Part also sets out circumstances in which a licensable activity and qualifying club activity may be carried on.

Section 1 – Licensable activities and qualifying club activities

25. This section in subsection (1) lists four activities which are to be regulated by the provisions of the Act and which constitute licensable activities. These are: -

- the sale by retail of alcohol (see commentary on sections 191 and 192);
- the supply of alcohol by clubs;
- the provision of regulated entertainment (see commentary on Schedule 1); and
- the provision of late night refreshment (see commentary on Schedule 2).

26. In subsection (2), this section lists those licensable activities which, for the purposes of the Act, are "qualifying club activities" and which as a consequence may be carried on by qualifying clubs under a club premises certificate (see commentary on Part 4 of the Act). Qualifying club activities are: -

- the supply of alcohol by clubs to members for consumption on or off the premises;
- the sale by retail of alcohol by clubs to members' guests for consumption on the premises; and
- the provision of regulated entertainment by the club for its members and guests.

27. Subsection (1)(b) specifies as a licensable activity the supply of alcohol by or on behalf of a club to or to the order of its members. This is necessary due to the fact that alcohol

in possession of a club will belong to its members and in terms of its further distribution to the members there will be no sale by retail. However, a sale by retail will take place in relation to purchases by guests of members.

28. Some bodies which call themselves "clubs" are in fact not within the ownership or control of their members. In such cases, any supplies of alcohol to members are sales by retail. Subsection (3) ensures that the references in the Act to the supply of alcohol by clubs to members do not include supplies by such clubs.

29. Finally, in subsection (7), the section refers forward to sections 173, 174 and 175 in Part 9 of the Act which provide that certain activities which would otherwise fall within subsection (1) are not licensable activities for the purposes of the Act (see commentary on Part 9).

Section 2 - Authorisation for licensable activities and qualifying club activities

30. Subsections (1) and (2) provide that a licensable activity may be carried on under and in accordance with a premises licence (see commentary on Part 3), a temporary event notice (see commentary on Part 5), or, if it is also a qualifying club activity, under and in accordance with a club premises certificate (see commentary on Part 4). By virtue of section 136 the carrying on of a licensable activity otherwise than in accordance with a premises licence, club premises certificate or temporary event notice is an offence.

31. Subsection (3) provides that more than one authorisation (that is, a premises licence, a club premises certificate or a temporary event notice) can cover the same premises. This enables, for example, a qualifying club that wishes to provide entertainment to members of the public on certain days to hold both a club premises certificate to cover its normal operation and a premises licence, to authorise the provision of entertainment, in respect of the same premises. Where there is more than one authorisation, they may be held by the same person or different people.

PART 2: Licensing authorities

General

32. Part 2 lists the bodies which are to be licensing authorities under the Act, describes the licensing objectives which the licensing authority must promote, and places an obligation on licensing authorities to publish a statement of licensing policy.

33. It also sets out the requirement for a licensing authority to establish a licensing committee and covers the delegation of licensing functions to licensing committees, sub-committees or officers of the licensing authority. The sections also cover the obligation to maintain a licensing register.

Section 3 - Licensing authorities

34. This section lists the bodies which for the purposes of the Act will act as licensing authorities. Subsection (2) describes the geographical area in which the authority will act.

Section 4 - General duties of licensing authorities

35. This section sets out the licensing objectives that must be promoted by the licensing authority in carrying out its duties. These are: -

- the prevention of crime and disorder;
- public safety;
- the prevention of public nuisance;
- the protection of children from harm.

36. The four licensing objectives aim to ensure that the carrying on of licensable activities on or from premises is done in the public interest. The third licensing objective, the prevention of public nuisance, will not extend to every activity which annoys another person but will cover behaviour which, when balanced against the public interest, is found to be unacceptable. The fourth licensing objective relates to harm to children beyond matters relating to physical safety.

37. Subsection (3) provides that when discharging its functions, the licensing authority must have regard to its policy framework document under section 5 and to any guidance issued by the Secretary of State (section 182).

*Section 5 - **Statement of licensing policy***

38. This section requires each licensing authority to determine and publish a statement of its licensing policy every three years. The first three-year period will begin with a day appointed by the Secretary of State. Subsection (3) lists those whom the licensing authority must consult in preparing its licensing policy; these include the police, the local fire authority, people who represent holders of premises and personal licences and club premises certificates, and people representative of local businesses and residents. Schedule 8 makes transitional provision requiring holders of those representing licensees under the existing licensing regimes to be consulted until the new regime is in force. Subsection (4) imposes a duty on an authority to keep its licensing policy under review. Any revisions to it, following consultation with those listed in subsection (3), must be published. Subsection (7) provides that the Secretary of State may make regulations relating to the formation of licensing policy and the publication of licensing statements.

*Section 6 - **Licensing Committee***

39. This section requires each licensing authority (with the exception of those which cover only the Inner and Middle Temples which consist, in each case, of only one person) to establish a licensing committee of between ten and fifteen members of the authority.

*Section 7 - **Exercise and delegation of functions***

40. Subsections (1) and (2) of this section provide that the licensing committee will discharge all of the authority's licensing functions, except for the function of the determination and publication of its statement of licensing policy.

41. Subsection (3) provides that the authority may decide that its licensing committee must also discharge additional functions of the authority that are related to its licensing functions. If a licensing authority chooses to discharge such related functions itself rather than to arrange for the licensing committee to discharge them, it must consider any relevant report prepared by the licensing committee before acting in any such matter (unless it is urgent). This ensures that the licensing committee will have an input into any matter relating to the authority's licensing functions.

42. Subsections (5) to (8) provide that in cases where a matter concerns other functions in addition to licensing functions, a licensing authority may choose to refer the matter either to its licensing committee (having first consulted it) or to another of its committees. If the latter course is followed, then in considering the matter, that committee must consider any report unless the matter is urgent) prepared by the licensing committee. If the former course is followed the licensing committee must, in considering the matter, consider any report about the matter prepared by any of the of the authority's other committees (again, unless the matter is urgent).

43. Subsection (9) makes provision that if a licensing committee is unable to discharge its functions because some of its members are prevented from considering or voting on a matter – for example, if they are disqualified under the licensing authority's standing orders because they have a financial interest in the matter – then the matter is instead

referred back to the licensing authority for it to discharge its functions in relation to the matter.

44. Subsection (10) disapplies the provisions in the section with respect to the Inner Temple and the Middle Temple with the result that in those cases the licensing authority will discharge all its licensing functions.

*Section 8 - **Requirement to keep a register***

45. Subsection (1) provides that each licensing authority must maintain a register which records details of the authorisations it issues, the temporary event notices it receives, other notices and applications to it as set out in Schedule 3, and any other information which the Secretary of State prescribes. Under subsection (2) the Secretary of State is given the power to make regulations as to how that register must be maintained. Subsections (3) to (5) provide that the information contained in the register must be made available for inspection by the public during office hours, free of charge, and that a copy of that information must be supplied on request (for a fee). Subsections (6) and (7) make provision for the Secretary of State to arrange, through administrative action, for the establishment of one or more central registers, in which case the licensing authorities may be required to pay for the cost of such arrangements.

*Section 9 - **Proceedings of licensing committee***

46. By virtue of the provision of this section, a licensing committee may form one or more sub-committees, each comprising three members of the committee. The Secretary of State is given the power to make regulations relating to the committees and sub-committees' proceedings, public access to their meetings, publicity, agendas and records. Otherwise, licensing committees may regulate their own procedure and that of their sub-committees.

*Section 10 - **Sub-delegation of functions by licensing committee etc.***

47. Subsection (1) provides that a licensing committee may sub-delegate the exercise of its functions to a sub-committee of the licensing committee, or to an officer of the licensing authority. Subsection (2) provides that in turn, the sub-committee can delegate functions to such an officer. Subsection (5) provides that such a delegation will, however, be subject to any direction made by the licensing committee. Subsection (3) provides that more than one such sub-committee or officer can discharge the same functions at the same time: thus, for example, a busy licensing committee which is faced with a high volume of licence applications could arrange for a number of licensing sub-committees to deal with them in parallel. However, subsection (4) sets out certain functions which may not be delegated to an officer. These are functions in respect of which representations or objections have been made and with which it is appropriate for the licensing committee or one of its licensing sub-committees to deal.

PART 3: Premises licences

General

48. This Part of the Act provides for a single licensing system for all premises used for licensable activities (see note on Part 1 for description of licensable activities). The 'relevant licensing authority' (see section 12) is to consider applications for premises licences.

49. Under the system established by the Act, an applicant for a premises licence will submit an operating schedule setting out certain details about the activities to be carried out on or from the premises. Where no relevant representations are made by responsible authorities (the police, fire authority, health and safety agency, etc) or interested parties (local residents and businesses), the licensing authority must grant the licence application, subject to certain mandatory conditions (see sections 19, 20 and 21).

50. If relevant representations are received, the licensing authority must, unless specified persons agree, convene a hearing and consider the representations. This consideration may result in the rejection of the licence application in whole or in part, or the attachment of conditions to the licence that relate to the promotion of one or more of the licensing objectives.

Section 11 - ***Premises licence***

51. For the purposes of the Act, a premises licence is defined in the section as a licence which authorises the use of specified premises for the carrying on of one or more licensable activities (see sections 1 and 2).

Section 12 - ***The relevant licensing authority***

52. This section provides that for the purposes of premises licences, the relevant licensing authority for any premises is the authority in whose area the premises are situated (or mainly situated). If premises straddle two or more areas equally, applicants can nominate one of the licensing authorities in question to act as the relevant licensing authority. The effect of this section is to identify the authority which will carry out licensing functions in relation to premises licences.

Section 13 - ***Authorised persons, interested parties and responsible authorities***

53. This section defines the terms 'authorised persons', 'interested parties' and 'responsible authorities'. The significance of designation as an 'authorised person' is that it confers a role in the inspection of premises in connection with their use for licensable activities (see in particular sections 57 and 59). An interested party or responsible authority may make representations to a licensing authority in relation to the application for the grant, variation or review of a premises licence.

Section 14 – ***Meaning of 'supply of alcohol'***

54. This section defines for the purposes of Part 3 the 'supply of alcohol' as sale by retail or the supply by or on behalf of a club to its members (see paragraph 27 above).

Section 15 – ***Meaning of 'designated premises supervisor'***

55. This section defines the term 'designated premises supervisor' as the individual who is specified in a premises licence as fulfilling the role of 'premises supervisor' for those premises. A 'designated premises supervisor' is required in every case where the premises licence authorises the supply of alcohol, and no supply of alcohol may be made on the premises unless there is a designated premises supervisor in possession of a personal licence (see section 19).

Section 16 – ***Applicant for premises licence***

56. This section lists the categories of persons who may apply for a premises licence in respect of any premises. The principal category is anyone who carries on or proposes to carry on a business involving licensable activities on the premises. This will cover any individual (aged at least 18) or business which wishes to carry on, on a commercial basis, the sale of alcohol, the supply of alcohol by a club, or the provision of regulated entertainment (see Schedule 1) or of late night refreshment (see Schedule 2).

57. The section also provides that the following may apply for a premises licence: a person exercising a statutory function (for example, a local authority); a person exercising any function by virtue of the Royal prerogative (for example, a body exercising functions by virtue of a royal charter); recognised clubs (see note on Part 4); charities; educational institutions; health bodies in the public and private sector; the police; and any other category of person prescribed in regulations made by the Secretary of State.

Section 17 - Application for a premises licence

58. Subsections (1) to (3) provide that applications for a premises licence should be made, in the form prescribed in regulations made by the Secretary of State, to the relevant licensing authority, and must be accompanied by an operating schedule, a plan of the premises and (if the application proposes that the licence will authorise the supply of alcohol) a form containing the consent of the individual whom it is proposed will be specified in the licence as the designated premises supervisor.

59. Subsection (4) provides that the operating schedule must set out various details relating to the operation of the premises when carrying on licensable activities, including the licensable activities to be carried out, the proposed hours of opening etc, the duration of the licence (if it is to have a fixed term), details about the individual (if any) who is to act as the designated premises supervisor, details of whether alcohol is to be supplied (if at all) for on-sales, off-sales or both, and a statement of how the applicant intends to promote the licensing objectives (for instance, the arrangements to be put in place to prevent crime and disorder, such as door security). The significance of the operating schedule is that if the application for the premises licence is approved, it will be incorporated into the licence itself and will set out the permitted activities and the limitations on them. As a consequence, it is the applicant who will decide, subject to the determination of applications by the authority, the nature and the extent of the activities and the conditions relating to the carrying on of the activities.

60. Subsection (5) provides that the Secretary of State must make regulations setting out how applications are to be advertised, and specifying when interested parties and responsible authorities can make representations to the authority.

Section 18 – Determination of application for premises licence

61. Subsections (1) and (2) provide that unless relevant representations are made in respect of an application for a premises licence, a licensing authority will be required to grant a licence in accordance with the application if it is duly made. That licence will be subject to conditions consistent with those listed by the applicant in the operating schedule, and subject to the mandatory conditions set out in sections 19, 20 and 21.

62. Subsection (3), together with subsections (6) to (8), provides that where relevant representations are made, licensing authorities are required to hold a hearing. In order for representations to be 'relevant' they must have been made by an interested party or a responsible authority (see the definitions in section 13, paragraph 53 above) and they must relate to the likely effect of the grant of the licence on the promotion of the licensing objectives. Representation relating to the identity of the premises supervisor may only be made by the police (see subsections (6)(c) and (9)) and must meet the requirements of subsection (9)(b). If the representations are made by an interested party there is a further requirement that the licensing authority does not consider them to be frivolous or vexatious. If it does the authority is to explain its decision to the person who made the representations.

63. The need for a hearing can be dispensed with by agreement of the authority, the applicant for the licence and all of the parties who have made relevant representations.

64. Subsection (4) provides that when a hearing is held (or dispensed with as indicated above), the licensing authority must, if it considers it necessary for the promotion of the licensing objectives, attach conditions to any licence granted, rule out any of the licensable activities applied for, refuse to specify a premises supervisor, or reject the application. For example, a licensing authority might decide to remove the playing of amplified recorded music after 11pm from the scope of the licence applied for by a tenant of a pub in the middle of a quiet residential area, or it might prohibit the admittance of under-18s to premises where adult entertainment is provided. If the authority takes the view that none of the foregoing steps is required to promote the licensing objectives it must grant the licence in the terms sought by the applicant.

65. Subsection (10) provides that a licensing authority may, within the same licence, impose different conditions on different parts of the premises, or impose different conditions in relation to different licensable activities.

*Section 19 - **Mandatory conditions where licence authorises supply of alcohol***

66. By virtue of this section some conditions are mandatory in respect of premises licences. The licensing authority will be required to attach to any premises licence authorising the supply of alcohol the conditions that at any time when such supplies under the premises licence are made

- there must be a 'designated premises supervisor' who is the holder of a valid personal licence, and
- every supply of alcohol under the premises licence must be made by a personal licence holder (although not necessarily by the designated premises supervisor) or an individual authorised by a personal licence holder.

*Section 20 – **Mandatory condition: exhibition of films***

67. Where a premises licence authorises the exhibition of a film this section makes it mandatory for a condition to be included in the premises licence requiring the admission of children to films to be restricted in accordance with recommendations given either by a body designated under section 4 of the Video Recordings Act 1984 or by the licensing authority itself. When the Act was passed the only body designated under section 4 of the Video Recordings Act 1984 was the British Board of Film Classification.

*Section 21 – **Mandatory condition: door supervision***

68. This section applies where the provision of door supervision is a requirement of the premises licence. It requires the licence to provide that anyone carrying out such a security function must be licensed by the Security Industry Authority established under the Private Security Industry Act 2001. Subsection (2) specifies some exceptions to this requirement (e.g. theatres). The provisions of the Private Security Industry Act 2001 are amended by paragraph 118 of Schedule 6 to the Act.

*Section 22 – **Prohibited conditions: plays***

69. Under this section, in the case of any premises licence authorising the performance of a play (see Schedule 1), licensing authorities will not be able to attach conditions relating to the nature of the play performed or the manner of its performance, unless they are justified as a matter of public safety. This section reproduces for England and Wales the effect of section 1(2) of the Theatres Act 1968.

*Section 23 – **Grant or rejection of application***

70. A licensing authority which grants or refuses a premises licence is required through this section to notify its decision to the applicant, to any person who made relevant representations and to the chief officer of police for the relevant area. If the application is granted, the licensing authority must also notify those parties of any steps it took in response to relevant representations and its reasons for taking or not taking the steps available. It must issue the licence and a summary of it to the applicant. If the application is rejected, the licensing authority must notify those parties of the reasons for its decision.

*Section 24 – **Form of licence and summary***

71. This section makes provision for a premises licence and the summary of it to be in a form prescribed in regulations made by the Secretary of State. Subsection (2) lists the basic requirements which those regulations must include as to the information to

be included in a premises licence. Under section 57, the summary must be displayed prominently at the relevant premises.

Section 25 - *Theft, loss, etc. of premises licence or summary*

72. Subsection (1) provides that a premises licence holder may apply to the licensing authority for a copy of the premises licence if it has been lost, stolen, damaged or destroyed. Subsection (3) provides that if the licensing authority is satisfied of the veracity of such an application, it must then issue a certified copy of the licence. Where a licence has been lost or stolen, there is an additional requirement that the licence holder must have reported this to the police. A fee may be prescribed for the issue of replacement documents. Subsection (5) provides that the provisions in the Act will apply to the issued copy of the premises licence as they applied to the original licence. This section applies in relation to the summary of the licence as it applies to the licence.

Section 26 – *Period of validity of premises licence*

73. This section makes provision that, unless it has been granted only for a limited period, the premises licence will last until it is surrendered or revoked. Subsection (2) provides that if a premises licence is suspended, it will not have effect during periods of suspension.

Section 27 – *Death, incapacity, insolvency etc of licence holder*

74. This section provides that a premises licence will lapse if the holder dies, becomes mentally incapable or insolvent, in the case of a company is dissolved, or in the case of a club ceases to be a recognised club. Insolvency, is relevant to individuals or companies and is widely defined to include, among other things, voluntary arrangements, bankruptcy, administration and administrative receivership. Subsection (2) provides that the lapse of a licence is subject to the possibility of it being reinstated under section 47 or 50.

Section 28 – *Surrender of premises licence*

75. This section provides that a licence holder may voluntarily surrender a premises licence by returning it to the licensing authority accompanied by a notice of surrender. If it is impractical to return the licence (e.g. where it has been lost), a statement to that effect must be sent with the notice of surrender. A premises licence ceases to have effect when the authority receives the notice of surrender. Subsection (4) makes reference to the fact that, in certain circumstances, surrendered licences can be reinstated (see section 50).

Section 29 – *Application for a provisional statement where premises being built, etc.*

76. Subsections (1) and (2) provide that in relation to premises which are being or are about to be constructed, extended or altered for use for licensable activities a person interested in the premises (in the case of an individual there is the requirement that the person is 18 or over) may apply to the licensing authority for a 'provisional statement'. A provisional statement is a statement issued by the authority in accordance with section 31 (see paragraph 78 below). Subsection (4) provides that any such application may be required to be in a form prescribed by the Secretary of State and accompanied by a fee. Subsection (6) provides that the application must also be accompanied by a schedule of works, which sets out details of the premises concerned, of the licensable activities intended to be carried on there and of the planned construction or alteration works (with plans). The effect of the section is to establish a mechanism whereby those engaged in or about to engage in construction or development work at premises to be used for licensable activities, or already used for those activities, can obtain a certain degree of assurance about their potential trading conditions. By obtaining a provisional statement they can receive, at an early stage, a statement describing the likely effect of

the intended licensable activities on the licensing objectives and an indication of the prospects of any future application for a premises licence.

*Section 30 – **Advertisement of application for provisional statement***

77. This section provides that regulations must require applications for provisional statements to be advertised in the prescribed manner to give responsible authorities and interested parties, including local residents, the opportunity to make representations about the application. Those regulations may also require any such advertisement to contain a statement, in wording set by the regulations, to make it clear that people will be precluded from subsequently objecting to the grant of a premises licence for the premises concerned if they could have made the same objection when the provisional statement was sought.

*Section 31 – **Determination of application for provisional statement***

78. Subsections (1) and (2) provide that unless relevant representations are made in respect of an application for a provisional statement, a licensing authority will be required to issue a provisional statement stating that no relevant representations have been made.

79. Subsection (3), together with subsections (6) and (7), provide that where relevant representations are made licensing authorities are required to hold a hearing. In order for representations to be 'relevant' they must have been made by an interested party or a responsible authority (see the definitions in section 13) and they must relate to the likely effect on the licensing objectives if a premises licence were to be granted in the form sought if the premises were constructed or altered in the way proposed in the schedule of works (see section 29). If the representations are made by an interested party there is a further requirement that the licensing authority does not consider them to be frivolous or vexatious. If it does, the authority is to explain its decision to the person who made the representations. The need for a hearing can be dispensed with by agreement of the authority, the applicant for the provisional statement and all of the parties who have made relevant representations.

80. When a hearing is held (or dispensed with as indicated above), the licensing authority must decide whether, if the premises were constructed or altered in the way proposed in the schedule of works and if a premises licence was sought for those premises, it would consider it necessary for the promotion of the licensing objectives to attach conditions to the licence, to rule out any of the licensable activities applied for, to refuse to accept the person specified as premises supervisor, or to reject the application. The licensing authority must then notify its decision (together with its reasons for considering that it would be necessary to impose any condition or restriction in respect of a premises licence or reject an application for a premises licence) to the applicant, the police and any person who has made relevant representations about the application.

*Section 32 – **Restriction on making representations following provisional statement***

81. By virtue of this section, in cases where a premises licence is later sought for premises in relation to which a provisional statement has been issued, interested parties and responsible authorities will not be able to make representations on such applications in respect of matters upon which representations could have been made by them when the provisional statement was applied for. Subsection (3) provides that this restriction will not apply if a person who wishes to make those representations has a reasonable excuse for not having made those representations at the time of the application for the provisional statement, or if there has been a material change in the circumstances relating to those premises or the vicinity of those premises since that time. For example, a person may have been confined to hospital during the period in which representations could have been made in circumstances where arrangements could not have been put in place for representations to be made.

Section 33 – Notification of change of name or address.

82. This section places a duty on the holder of a premises licence to notify the licensing authority of any change of name or address of the premises licence holder or of the designated premises supervisor (unless the designated premises supervisor has already done so in accordance with subsection (4)). Such notification of a change of the licence holder's name or address or that of the designated premises supervisor must be accompanied by the licence (unless that is impracticable, when a statement must be provided) and by any fee that may have been prescribed. Notification of a change of the designated premises supervisor's name or address may be made by the designated premises supervisor under subsection (4) (in which case he must notify the licence holder). Failure to provide the required notifications is an offence.

Section 34 - Application to vary premises licence

Section 35 - Determination of application under section 34 and

Section 36 - Supplementary provision about determinations under section 35

83. Under these sections a premises licence holder can apply, in the prescribed form and manner, to vary that licence in any way, other than to change the designated premises supervisor (for which there is a separate procedure (see section 37)), to extend the time for which the licence has effect (if it is time limited) or to vary substantially the premises to which it relates. In general the ability to apply for a variation of a premises licence under these sections will concern variation of the conditions attaching to the licence or of the authorised licensable activities. Any such application may be subject to a fee and is subject to regulations under section 17 relating to advertising requirements. The application must also be accompanied by the premises licence (unless that is impracticable when a statement explaining why must be provided).

84. By virtue of section 35, the authority must make the variation as applied for, subject to the mandatory conditions, unless relevant representations are made, in which case a hearing must be held. In order for representations to be 'relevant' they must have been made by an interested party or a responsible authority (see the definitions in section 13) and they must relate to the likely effect on the promotion of the licensing objectives if the application were to be granted. If the representations are made by an interested party there is a further requirement that the licensing authority does not consider them to be frivolous or vexatious. If it thinks they are, it must explain its decision to the person who made the representations. The need for a hearing can be dispensed with by agreement of the authority, the applicant for the variation and all of the parties who have made relevant representations.

85. In any case where relevant representations have been made, subsection (3) of section 35 provides that the licensing authority must, if it considers it necessary for the promotion of the licensing objectives (see section 4), modify the conditions of the licence or reject the application for variation (in whole or in part). If the licensing authority does not consider it necessary to modify the licence or reject the application it will grant the variation in the terms sought. The authority must notify its decision to the applicant, the police and any person who has made relevant representations, and must give reasons for its decision. A variation of a premises licence may impose different conditions on different parts of the premises, or impose different conditions in relation to different licensable activities. The provisions in these sections follow closely the procedure to apply in respect of an original application for a premises licence (see paragraph 58 above).

Section 37 – Application to vary licence to specify individual as premises supervisor

86. Subsections (1) to (3) provide that a premises licence holder can apply to name a person in the licence as the premises supervisor or substitute a different person for the person

currently named. Any such application may be required to be in a form prescribed by the Secretary of State and to be accompanied by a fee. The application must also be accompanied by a form of consent given by the proposed new premises supervisor, and by the premises licence or the relevant part of the licence or a statement as to why the licence or part cannot be submitted. Subsection (4) provides that the applicant must notify the police and the existing designated premises supervisor, if there is one, of the application. Subsections (5) and (6) provide that the chief officer of police can object to the variation if he believes there are exceptional circumstances whereby the grant of the application to specify a new premises supervisor would undermine the crime prevention objective, and if so he must provide reasons for his decision within 14 days.

Section 38 – ***Circumstances in which*** *section 37* ***application given interim effect***

87. An application to vary a premises licence so as to name a different premises supervisor may be given immediate effect (that is, from the time that the application is received by the licensing authority) if the premises licence holder requests it at the time he makes an application under section 37. This section enables the holder of a premises licence to continue the supply of alcohol if, for example, the existing premises supervisor is suddenly indisposed or unable to work. If the application is rejected, the licence reverts to the form it took before the application was made.

Section 39 – ***Determination of*** *section 37* ***application***

88. By virtue of this section the relevant licensing authority must grant the application to vary the designated premises supervisor except where the chief officer of police for the area gives notice that to do so would undermine the crime prevention objective, in which case a hearing must be held. The need for a hearing can be dispensed with by agreement of the authority, the applicant for the variation and the police.

89. In any case where the police have given notice of objection under section 37 (5), the licensing authority must, if it considers it necessary for the promotion of the licensing objectives (see section 4), reject the application for this variation. In any other case the variation must be granted.

90. The authority must notify its decision to the applicant, the police and the proposed new designated premises supervisor, and must give reasons for its decision.

Section 40 – ***Duty of applicant following determination under*** *section 39*

91. If an application to vary the designated premises supervisor is granted, by virtue of this section the premises licence holder must notify the person (if any) who is being replaced as such supervisor. Failure to do so will be an offence.

Section 41 – ***Request to be removed as designated premises supervisor***

92. A person who wishes to cease acting as designated premises supervisor may give notice under this section. If this person is also the premises licence holder, his notice must be accompanied by the premises licence (unless that is impracticable when he must give a statement of reason as to why this is the case). If he is not the premises licence holder, he must provide the licence holder with a copy of the notice and notify the licence holder that he must send the premises licence to the relevant authority. Failure by the licence holder to submit the licence will be an offence. An effect of this section is that whenever a person stops acting as a designated premises supervisor, the licensing authority will be informed of it and can make the appropriate change in the licensing register. By virtue of subsections (7) and (8) the designated premises supervisor will cease to be such either at the time the licensing authority receives an application or the time specified in the notice if that is later.

Section 42 – Application for transfer of premises licence

93. Subsections (1) and (2) set out those people or bodies who may apply for the transfer of a premises licence. These are the same as the people and bodies who may apply to be granted a premises licence under section 16. Any such application may be required to be in a form prescribed by the Secretary of State and to be accompanied by a fee. The application must also be accompanied by the premises licence (unless that is impracticable and then the applicant must state the reasons why this is the case). Subsection (5) provides that the applicant must notify the application to the chief officer of police for the area. The police can object to the transfer if they believe there are exceptional circumstances whereby the grant of the application would undermine the crime prevention objective, and if so they must notify the licensing authority and provide reasons for the objection within 14 days.

Section 43 – Circumstances in which transfer application given interim effect

94. By virtue of this section a person applying for the transfer of a premises licence may request that it be given immediate effect (that is, that it takes effect from the time that the application is received by the licensing authority). Such an application generally requires the consent of the holder of the premises licence. But no consent is required if the applicant can show that he has taken all reasonable steps to obtain that consent and that he is in a position to use the premises straightaway for the licensable activities authorised by the licence. An authority must provide reasons for any decision to refuse to exempt an applicant from the requirement for consent. The effect of this section is to allow licensable activities to be carried on, at the premises, without interruption, pending the determination of an application for a transfer. The section allows for the possibility of a transfer being given interim effect even where the transferor has not given consent because in some circumstances he may be indisposed or unable to give consent, or a conflict may exist between the existing licence holder and others which does not concern the carrying on of the licensable activities for the purposes of the Act. If the application is rejected, the applicant ceases to be treated as the holder of the licence under this section and the licence reverts to the person who held it before the application was made.

Section 44 – Determination of transfer application

95. Where a person applies for a premises licence to be transferred to him, this section provides that the licensing authority may not consider the application unless

- the transfer application has been given immediate effect under section 43,
- the existing licence holder has agreed to the transfer, or
- the applicant has been exempted from the need to obtain that consent. An applicant will be so exempted if he can show that he has taken all reasonable steps to obtain that consent and that he is in a position to use the premises straightaway for the licensable activities authorised by the licence. An authority must provide reasons for any decision to refuse to exempt an applicant.

96. Subsection (5) provides that if the police have notified the licensing authority of objections under section 42, the authority must hold a hearing to consider the application for transfer, and, if it considers it necessary for the promotion of the crime prevention objective (see section 4), must reject the application. The need for a hearing can be dispensed with by agreement of the authority, the applicant for the transfer and the police. The section provides, in subsection (2), that in all other cases the authority must grant the application for transfer.

*Section 45 – **Notification of determination under** section 44*

97. By virtue of this section the licensing authority must notify its decision to the applicant and to the police, and in any case where the police gave notice under section 42 the authority must give reasons for its decision to grant or reject the application. The authority must also notify its decision to the person who was the licence holder before the application for transfer was made or, where applicable, before it was given interim effect.

*Section 46 – **Duty to notify designated premises supervisor of transfer***

98. An applicant for the transfer of a premises licence pursuant to sections 42 and 43 must under this section notify the designated premises supervisor (if any) specified in that licence of his application and, if the application is successful, of the transfer of the premises licence to him. Failure to do so is an offence.

*Section 47 – **Interim authority notice following death etc of licence holder***

99. In the initial seven days after the lapse of a premises licence due to the death, mental incapacity or insolvency of a premises licence holder, those with a prescribed interest in the relevant premises or connected to the licence holder (by virtue of being the licence holder's personal representative, having an enduring power of attorney in respect of the individual or acting as insolvency practitioner), under this section can give an interim authority notice to the relevant licensing authority. But no notice can be given if application for a transfer of the premises licence under section 50 has already been made (see paragraph 102 below). Any such notice may be required to be in a form prescribed by the Secretary of State and to be accompanied by a fee. By virtue of subsection (6) the effect of such a notice will be to reinstate the lapsed premises licence, and for the person who gave that notice to become the licence holder, from the time the authority receives the notice for two months, or until terminated by the person who gave notice, unless a successful transfer application is made to the relevant authority within that time. The reinstated licence will also lapse if the police are not notified of the giving of the notice within the initial seven day period (see subsection (7)). A person who gives an interim authority notice becomes the holder of the licence for the interim authority period. Subsection (8) makes it clear that, notwithstanding this, he may apply for the licence to be transferred to him permanently.

*Section 48 – **Cancellation of interim authority notice following police objections***

100. Subsections (1) and (2) provide that the police can object within 48 hours of being notified of an interim authority notice, but they can do so only where they believe that exceptional circumstances mean that a failure to cancel the notice would undermine the crime prevention objective. Subsections (3) to (6) provide that in such cases, the authority must hold a hearing to decide whether or not to cancel the notice. The need for a hearing can be dispensed with by agreement of the authority, the police and the person who has given the interim authority notice. If the authority considers it necessary for the promotion of the crime prevention objective (see section 4), it must cancel the interim authority notice. If it does so the licence will again lapse. A cancellation must be notified to the police and to the person who gave the interim authority notice, together with the authority's reasons for its decision. Subsection (6) (the lapse of the licence) is expressed to be subject to reinstatement in the case of an appeal. Subsection (7) provides that the authority cannot cancel an interim authority notice after a time when a transfer application has been made which provides for the transfer to have interim effect (sections 42 and 43).

*Section 49 – **Supplementary provision about interim authority notice***

101. Subsections (1) to (3) provide that when a licensing authority receives an interim authority notice, it must send the person who sent that notice a copy of the premises

licence (and summary) in the form it was in immediately prior to the licence lapsing, save that it will specify that person as the licence holder. Subsections (4) to (6) provide that anyone who became the licence holder under section 47 must notify the designated premises supervisor specified in the licence (if any) of the interim authority notice. It will be an offence to fail to do so, without reasonable excuse.

Section 50 – ***Reinstatement of licence on transfer following death etc of holder***

102. Where a premises licence lapses under section 27 (death, incapacity or insolvency of the holder etc.) or by its surrender, but no interim authority notice has effect (as defined by subsection (2)), a person who may apply for the grant of a premises licence under section 16(1) may apply within seven days of the lapse for the transfer of the licence to him. This will cause the licence to be reinstated from the point at which the transfer application is received by the licensing authority. Subsection (3) provides that a reinstatement will only occur if the transfer application is one which is to have immediate effect under section 43. If the application is rejected or withdrawn, however, the licence lapses again.

Section 51 – ***Application for review of premises licence***

103. Subsections (1) to (3) make provision for an interested party or responsible authority to apply, in such manner and form as may be prescribed and subject to the regulations that must be made by the Secretary of State about requirements as to notification and advertisements, to a relevant licensing authority for a review of the premises licence. For example, a local resident may consider that the measures taken by the licensee to prevent public nuisance are insufficient and request that they be reviewed. Similarly, the police may consider that the measures put in place to prevent crime and disorder are not being effective and need to be reviewed. Subsections (4) to (7) provide that the authority can at any stage reject a ground for review in an application unless it is relevant to at least one of the licensing objectives, or (if the application is made by an interested party) if it is frivolous, vexatious or repetitious (namely, identical or substantially similar to a ground for review already considered by the authority in a previous review, or in the determination of the application for grant of the licence, and a reasonable period has not passed since that time.) Under subsection (6) if a licensing authority rejects a ground for a review on the basis that it is frivolous or vexatious it must notify the applicant of its reasons.

Section 52 – ***Determination of application for review***

104. By virtue of this section, the authority must hold a hearing to consider and determine any application for review and any relevant representations made in respect of it. In order for representations to be 'relevant' they must have been made by the holder of the premises licence, an interested party or a responsible authority (see the definitions in section 13) and they must relate to the licensing objectives. If the representations are made by an interested party there is a further requirement that the licensing authority does not consider them to be frivolous or vexatious. If it does, the authority is to explain its decision to the person who made the representations. The section provides that as a result of this review the authority must, if it considers it necessary for the promotion of the licensing objectives, either modify the conditions of the licence, exclude a licensable activity which the premises licence covers, remove the designated supervisor, suspend the licence for a period not exceeding 3 months or revoke the licence. If the licensing authority does not consider any of the steps to be necessary for the promotion of the licensing objectives, it will leave the licence untouched.

105. Subsection (10) requires the licensing authority to notify the outcome of a review and its reasons for so deciding to the licence holder, the applicant, the police and any person who has made relevant representations. Subsection (11) provides that the determination of an application for review will not take effect until any appeal has been disposed of,

or if there is no appeal at the end of the period within which an appeal may be brought (see Schedule 5).

*Section 53 – **Supplementary provision about review***

106. A local authority that is both the relevant licensing authority and a responsible authority – for example, where it carries out the functions of the local environmental health authority – may apply for a review in its capacity as a responsible authority and determine that application in its capacity as licensing authority.

*Section 54 – **Form etc of applications and notices under** Part 3*

107. This section provides that, in relation to any application or notice in Part 3, regulations made by the Secretary of State may prescribe its form, the manner in which it should be made or given, and any information and documents that must accompany the notice or application.

*Section 55 – **Fees***

108. By virtue of the exercise of the power under this section, premises licence holders may be required by regulations to pay an annual fee to the licensing authority, the amount and due date of which may be set by the Secretary of State. In addition, regulations may prescribe a fee in relation to any applications under Part 3 (other than applications for a review) or interim authority notices.

*Section 56 – **Licensing authority's duty to update licence document***

109. Subsection (1) requires the relevant licensing authority to amend a premises licence to reflect any determination by the authority in relation to the licence, the lapsing of the licence or the disposal of an appeal. This ensures that there is always an accurate record of the licence.

110. In most cases the licensing authority will have sent the appropriate licence (or part of a licence) to the licensing authority, but subsections (2) to (4) provide that the authority may require holders to produce licences or the appropriate parts of licences for this purpose. Failure to do so without reasonable excuse will be an offence.

*Section 57 – **Duty to keep and produce licence***

111. Under this section a premises licence holder must ensure that the licence or a certified copy is held on the premises to which it relates either by the licence holder or by an individual nominated for this purpose by the licence holder. A summary of the licence and notice of the individual responsible for the custody of the licence on the premises, if not the licence holder, must be displayed prominently on the premises. It will be an offence to fail to comply with these requirements or to fail to produce the licence or a certified copy to a constable or an authorised person (see section 13) on request. Subsection (9) provides that the requirements relate to the most up to date summary of the licence issued under section 23 or 56.

*Section 58 – **Provision supplementary to** section 57*

112. By virtue of this section, a copy of a premises licence or summary is to be certified as a true copy by either the relevant licensing authority, a solicitor or notary, or any other person the Secretary of State may prescribe. Subsection (3) provides that a certified copy will be presumed to be a true copy of the original unless the contrary is shown.

*Section 59 – **Inspection of premises before grant of licence, etc***

113. This section provides that a constable or an authorised person (see the definition in section 13) may enter the premises to which an application relates, before that

application has been determined, in order to assess the likely effect on the promotion of the licensing objectives of the grant of the application, or as the case may be, the effect of the activities authorised by a licence which is the subject of an application for review. In the case of an authorised person, evidence of authorisation to enter must be produced if requested. Where entry is sought in connection with an application for review both constables and authorised persons may use reasonable force to gain entry to premises if necessary. It is an offence under this section to obstruct an authorised person exercising these powers. It is already an offence under the Police Act 1996 to obstruct a constable in the course of his duties.

PART 4: Clubs

General

114. This Part provides for arrangements for qualifying clubs (as defined in section 61), (such as the British Legion, working men's or cricket or rugby clubs) which meet specified criteria to carry on certain licensable activities at their premises. In this Act such activities are called "qualifying club activities". Such clubs are treated differently from other venues because they carry on activities from private premises (to which access is accordingly restricted) and because alcohol and regulated entertainment are provided otherwise than for profit.

115. This Part establishes a system of club premises certificates, issued by the relevant licensing authority, which authorise a qualifying club to carry on qualifying club activities. Qualifying clubs have a special status under licensing law; clubs holding certificates will be exempted from the requirement for any member or employee to hold a personal licence to supply or sell alcohol to members or guests. The general offence of supplying alcohol to people under 18 applies in clubs as it does elsewhere (see commentary on Part 7 below).

116. Applications for club premises certificates, like those for premises certificates, will be made by submitting the required documents to the licensing authority (namely, the operating schedule, a plan of the premises and a copy of the club's rules). The operating schedule sets out the activities proposed to be undertaken, the planned hours of opening, and the arrangements the club proposes taking to promote the licensing objectives (see section 4).

117. An application for a club premises certificate is subject to provision about advertisement and representations, similar to that for an application for a premises licence (see paragraph 60 above).

*Section 60 – **Club premises certificate***

118. This section defines "club premises certificate" for the purposes of the Act.

*Section 61 – **Qualifying clubs***

119. This section provides that a club is a qualifying club, in relation to a qualifying club activity, if it satisfies the general conditions (see section 62) and if, in relation to the supply of alcohol to its members or their guests, it also satisfies the additional conditions (see section 64).

*Section 62 – **The general conditions***

120. This section sets out 5 general conditions for a club to be a qualifying club. They are that:

- nobody can be admitted as a member without an interval of at least two days after their nomination or application for membership;

- a person who is admitted as a member other than by prior nomination or application must wait at least two days before enjoying the privileges of membership;
- the club is established and conducted in good faith as a club (as to which, see section 63);
- the club has at least 25 members;
- no alcohol is supplied, or intended to be supplied, on the club premises except by or on behalf of the club.

*Section 63 – **Determining whether a club is established and conducted in good faith***

121. This section sets out the matters that must be taken into account in determining whether a club satisfies the condition of being established and conducted in good faith. These matters include restrictions on

- the club's freedom to purchase alcohol;
- how money or property belonging to the club is used;
- giving members information about the club's finances;
- the club's accounts; and
- the nature of its premises.

122. If a licensing authority determines that a club does not satisfy this condition, it must notify the club accordingly and give reasons for its decision.

*Section 64 – **The additional conditions for the supply of alcohol***

123. This section sets out the three additional conditions that a club must satisfy if it is to be a qualifying club in relation to the supply of alcohol to members and their guests. These conditions are that the purchase and supply of alcohol should be managed by a committee, that nobody should receive at the expense of the club a commission or percentage deriving from purchase of alcohol, and that nobody should receive a pecuniary benefit from the supply of alcohol by the club to its members or their guests.

*Section 65 – **Industrial and provident societies, friendly societies, etc.***

*Section 66 – **Miners' welfare institutes***

124. These sections provide that, for the purposes of the Act, registered industrial and provident societies, registered and incorporated friendly societies and miners' welfare institutes will be treated as satisfying certain of the general conditions and additional conditions for being a qualifying club if certain requirements relating to their constitution and management are met. The effect of the provisions of these sections is that such bodies may apply for a club premises certificate.

*Section 67 – **Associate members and their guests***

125. This section provides that references to club members' guests are to be taken to include associate members of the club, and associate members' guests. So such persons can have the benefit of licensable activities or qualifying club activities provided on club premises.

*Section 68 – **The relevant licensing authority***

126. For the purposes of this Part, the "relevant licensing authority" is the authority in whose area a club's premises are situated (or mainly situated). (If the premises straddle two or more areas equally, applicants can nominate one of the authorities in question to act as

the relevant licensing authority.) The effect of this section is to determine the authority to which an application for a club premises certificate may be made by a qualifying club.

*Section 69 – **Authorised persons, interested parties and responsible authorities***

127. This section defines the terms 'authorised persons', 'interested party' and 'responsible authority'. The significance of designation as an 'authorised person' is that it confers a role in the inspection of premises in connection with their use for licensable activities. An interested party or responsible authority may make representations to a licensing authority in relation to the grant, variation or review of a club premises certificate.

128. This Part also provides that applicants for club premises certificates must give notice to responsible authorities and advertise applications in a manner likely to bring them to the attention of the interested parties.

*Section 70 – **Other definitions relating to clubs***

129. This section defines 'secretary' for the purposes of this Part of the Act as any person performing the duties of a secretary.

*Section 71 – **Application for club premises certificate***

130. Subsections (1) to (4) provide that applications for a club premises certificate for premises which are occupied by and used for the purposes of a club may be made by a qualifying club to the relevant licensing authority (see section 68). Applications are to be made in the form prescribed in regulations made by the Secretary of State and accompanied by a fee similarly prescribed.

131. Subsection (5) provides that the operating schedule will set out various details relating to the operation of particular club premises. Those details include the qualifying club activities to be carried out, the proposed hours of those activities and other times when it is proposed that the premises will be open to members and their guests, whether, where the qualifying club activities include the supply of alcohol, the supplies will be for consumption on or off the premises or both and a statement of how it is intended to promote the licensing objectives. The significance of the operating schedule is that if the application for the club premises certificate is granted, the details will be incorporated into the certificate, which will set out the permitted activities and the limitations on them.

132. Subsection (6) provides that the Secretary of State must make regulations setting out how applications must be notified and advertised, and specifying when interested parties and responsible authorities can make representations to the authority.

*Section 72 – **Determination of application for club premises certificate***

133. Subsections (1) and (2) provide that unless relevant representations are made in respect of an application for a club premises certificate, a licensing authority must grant a certificate in accordance with any such application which is duly made. That certificate will be subject to conditions consistent with those included in the application by the applicant in the operating schedule, and subject to the mandatory conditions set out in sections 73 and 74.

134. Subsection (3), together with subsections (6) to (8), provides that where relevant representations are made, licensing authorities are required to hold a hearing. In order for representations to be 'relevant' they must have been made by an interested party or a responsible authority (see the definitions in section 69) and they must relate to the likely effect of the grant of the certificate on the promotion of the licensing objectives. If the representations are made by an interested party there is a further requirement that the licensing authority does not consider them to be frivolous or vexatious (but if it does, the authority is to explain its decision to the person who made the representations). The

need for a hearing can be dispensed with by agreement of the authority, the applicant for the certificate and all of the parties who have made relevant representations.

135. Subsection (4) provides that when a hearing is held (or dispensed with as indicated above), the licensing authority must, if it considers it necessary for the promotion of the licensing objectives, attach conditions to any certificate granted, rule out any of the qualifying club activities applied for, or reject the application. Otherwise the licensing authority will grant the certificate in the terms sought in the application (together with any mandatory conditions).

136. Subsection (10) provides that a licensing authority may, within the same certificate, impose different conditions on different parts of the premises, or impose different conditions in relation to different qualifying club activities.

*Section 73 – **Certificate authorising supply of alcohol for consumption off the premises***

By virtue of this section, a club premises certificate may authorise the supply of alcohol by a club to its members for consumption off the premises only in certain circumstances. The sale by retail of alcohol to a guest of a member for consumption off the premises is not a qualifying club activity.

By virtue of this section -

- A club premises certificate may not authorise the supply of alcohol for consumption off the premises unless it also authorises its supply to members for consumption on the premises
- A club premises certificate authorising the supply of alcohol for consumption off the premises must include three conditions. These are:
    - (i) the supply must be made at a time when the premises are open for the purposes of supplying alcohol, in accordance with the club premises certificate, to members of the club for consumption on the premises
    - (ii) any alcohol supplied for consumption off the premises must be in a sealed container
    - (iii) any supply of alcohol for consumption off the premises must be made to a member of the club in person.

*Section 74 – **Mandatory condition: exhibition of films***

137. Where a club premises certificate authorises the exhibition of a film this section makes it mandatory for a condition to be included in the certificate requiring the admission of children to films to be restricted in accordance with recommendations given either by a body designated under section 4 of the Video Recordings Act 1984 or by the licensing authority itself. When the Act was passed the only body designated under section 4 of the Video Recordings Act 1984 was the British Board of Film Classification.

*Section 75– **Prohibited conditions: associate members and their guests***

138. This section provides that no conditions attached to a club premises certificate may prevent the sale by retail of alcohol or the provision of regulated entertainment to associate members of the club or their guests, if those activities are permitted by the rules of the club.

*Section 76– **Prohibited conditions: plays***

139. Under this section, in the case of a club premises certificate authorising the performance of a play (see Schedule 1), licensing authorities will not be able to attach conditions relating to the nature of the play performed or the manner of its performance, unless they are justified as a matter of public safety. This section reproduces for England and Wales the effect of section 1(2) of the Theatres Act 1968.

Section 77 – Grant or rejection of application for club premises certificate

140. By virtue of this section a licensing authority which grants or refuses a club premises certificate must notify its decision to the applicant, to any person who made representations and to the chief officer of police for the area in which the premises are situated. If the application is granted, the licensing authority must also notify those parties of any steps it took in response to relevant representations and give its reasons. It must issue the club premises certificate, and a summary of that certificate, to the applicant. If the application is rejected, the licensing authority must notify those parties of the reasons for its decision.

Section 78 - Form of certificate and summary

141. This section makes provision for a club premises certificate and the summary of that certificate to be in a form prescribed in regulations made by the Secretary of State. Subsection (2) lists the basic requirements which those regulations must include as to the content of the certificate. Under section 94, the summary must be displayed at the relevant premises.

Section 79 – Theft, loss etc. of certificate or summary

142. Subsection (1) provides that a club may apply to the licensing authority for a copy of a club premises certificate or summary if that certificate or summary has been lost, stolen, damaged or destroyed. Subsection (3) provides that if the licensing authority is satisfied of the veracity of such an application, it must then issue a certified copy of that certificate. Where a certificate has been lost or stolen, there is an additional requirement that the club has reported this to the police. A fee may be prescribed for the issue of replacement documents. The Act applies in relation to a copy in the same way as it applies to the original.

Section 80 – Period of validity of club premises certificate

143. By virtue of this section a club premises certificate has effect until it is withdrawn (see section 88 and 90) or it lapses on surrender by the club (see section 81). Subsection (2) provides that a club premises certificate does not have effect during periods of suspension.

Section 81 - Surrender of club premises certificate

144. This section provides that a club may voluntarily surrender its club premises certificate by returning it to the authority accompanied by a notice of surrender. If it is impractical to return the certificate (e.g. where it has been lost), a statement to this effect must be sent with the notice of surrender. A club premises certificate lapses when the authority receives the notice of surrender.

Section 82 – Notification of change of name or alteration of rules of club

145. Under this section, the secretary of a club must notify the relevant licensing authority of any change in the club's name or its rules. Notification of such a change must be accompanied by the certificate (unless that is impracticable and then a statement of the reasons as to why that is the case must be provided) and any fee that may have been prescribed. The licensing authority must amend the club premises certificate to record any such change, but a certificate may not be amended under this section so as to change the premises to which it relates. Failure to notify the authority of such a change within 28 days is an offence.

Section 83 – Change of relevant registered address of a club

146. Under this section, the secretary of a club may notify the relevant licensing authority of any change in the club's address, and must do so if the club ceases to make use of

the address which it has given as its relevant registered address. Notification of such a change must be accompanied by the certificate (unless that is impracticable and then a statement of the reasons as to why this is the case must be provided) and any fee that may have been prescribed. The licensing authority must amend the club premises certificate to record any such change. Failure by a club to notify the authority of a change of address when it has to do so is an offence.

Section 84 – ***Application to vary club premises certificate***

Section 85 – ***Determination of application under*** *section 84* ***and***

Section 86 – ***Supplementary provision about applications under*** *section 84*

147. Under these sections a club can apply, in the prescribed form and manner, to vary its club premises certificate in any way other than to vary substantially the premises to which it relates. Any such application may be subject to the payment of a fee and is subject to regulations under section 71 relating to advertising requirements. The application must also be accompanied by the club premises certificate (unless that is impracticable, in which case a statement of reasons must be provided).

148. Under section 85 the licensing authority must make the variation as applied for unless relevant representations are made, in which case a hearing must be held. In order for representations to be 'relevant' they must have been made by an interested party or a responsible authority (see the definitions in section 69) and they must relate to the likely effect on the promotion of the licensing objectives if the application were to be granted. If the representations are made by an interested party there is a further requirement that the licensing authority does not consider them to be frivolous or vexatious (but if it does the authority is to explain its decision to the person who made the representations). The need for a hearing can be dispensed with by agreement of the authority, the applicant for the variation and all of the parties who have made relevant representations.

149. By virtue of subsection (3) of section 85, in any case where relevant representations have been made, the licensing authority must, if it considers it necessary for the promotion of the licensing objectives (see section 4), modify the conditions of the certificate or reject the application for variation. Otherwise, the licensing authority must grant the variation in the terms sought (subject to the mandatory conditions). The authority must notify its decision to the applicant, the police and any person who has made relevant representations, and must give reasons for its decision. A variation of a club premises certificate may impose different conditions on different parts of the premises, or impose different conditions in relation to different qualifying club activities.

Section 87 – ***Application for review of club premises certificate***

150. Subsections (1) to (3) make provision for an interested party, responsible authority or a member of the club in question to apply (in such manner and form as may be prescribed and subject to any regulations made about requirements as to notification and advertisements) to a licensing authority for a review of the club premises certificate. Subsections (4) to (7) provide that the authority can at any stage reject a ground for review in an application if it is not relevant to any of the licensing objectives, or (where the application is made by an interested party) if it is frivolous, vexatious or repetitious. (A ground for review is a repetitious if it is identical or substantially similar to a ground for review already considered by the authority in a previous review, or in the determination of the application for grant of the certificate, and a reasonable period has not passed since that time).

Section88 – Determination of application for review and

Section 89 – Supplementary provision about review

151. Under the provisions of these sections the licensing authority must hold a hearing to consider and determine the application for a review and any relevant representations made in respect of it. Having regard to those matters, the authority must, if it considers it necessary for the promotion of the licensing objectives modify the conditions of the certificate or the activities which it covers, suspend the authority of the certificate for a period not exceeding 3 months or revoke the certificate. Otherwise the certificate will not be altered.

152. Section 88 provides that for representations to be relevant they must relate to one or more of the licensing objectives and be made by the club, a responsible authority or an interested party. If made by an interested party, the authority must be satisfied that they are not frivolous or vexatious. If the authority considers that they are, it must inform the party making the representations of its decision. The authority must notify the applicant, the club, any person who made relevant representations and the police of its decision and its reasons.

153. A local authority that is both the relevant licensing authority and a responsible authority – for example, where it carries out the functions of the local environmental health authority – may apply for a review in its capacity as a responsible authority and determine that application.

Section 90 – Club ceasing to be a qualifying club

154. A club which ceases to meet the criteria set out at sections 61, 62 and 63 and 64 will have its certificate withdrawn by the licensing authority. Where a certificate is withdrawn because the club's membership has fallen below the required minimum (currently 25), the withdrawal will not have effect until three months after the authority gives notice and does not have effect if, by the end of those three months, the membership has risen to at least the required minimum.

155. A justice of the peace may issue a search warrant authorising a constable to enter club premises (if necessary using force) to search them if he is satisfied that a club holding a club premises certificate ceases to meet the criteria necessary to be a qualifying club and evidence of such fact may be obtained at the club premises.

Section 91 – Form etc. of applications and notices under Part 4

156. This section allows for the detail of the form, manner and content of applications, and any accompanying documents, to be set out in regulations.

Section 92 – Fees

157. Clubs may be required by regulations to pay an annual fee to the licensing authority, the amount and due date of which may be prescribed, or fees in relation to any applications (other than an application for a review) or notices made under this Part.

Section 93 – Duty to provide licensing authority with club premises certificate

158. A club must produce the certificate at the request of the licensing authority. Failure to do so without reasonable excuse is an offence.

Section 94 - Duty to keep and produce certificate

Section 95 - Provision supplementary to section 94

159. Clubs must ensure that the certificate is held on the relevant premises, and that a summary of the certificate and notice of the nominated individual responsible for it on

the premises are displayed prominently. Failure to comply with those provisions is an offence.

160. A police officer or authorised person (see section 69) may require production of the certificate; failure to produce it is an offence.

*Section 96 - **Inspection of premises before grant of certificate etc.***

161. This section makes provision for a constable authorised by the chief officer of police or an authorised person (see section 69) to enter premises to which an application for a club premises certificate relates, or to which an application for a variation or a review of the certificate relates and inspect those premises, having given the club 48 hours notice. It is an offence to obstruct an authorised person exercising the power this section confers. It is already an offence under the Police Act 1996 to obstruct a police officer in the course of his duty.

*Section 97 - **Other powers of entry and search***

162. This section provides that a constable may enter and search club premises where he has reasonable cause to believe that an offence in respect of controlled drugs has been, is being, or is about to be, committed there or there is likely to be a breach of the peace.

PART 5: Permitted temporary activities

163. Part 5 makes provision for a system that would allow individuals – "premises users" – to carry out licensable activities on a temporary basis (for a period not exceeding 96 hours), subject to various conditions and limits attaching to the number of events which may be permitted. Different limits apply depending on whether or not the person carrying out licensable activities holds a personal licence (see Part 6) and the frequency of use of the premises.

164. Examples of circumstances under which an individual might make use of the arrangements could include:

- where a **personal licence holder** wishes to carry out one or more licensable activities at premises not covered by a premises licence relating to those activities. For example, a publican may be engaged to run a temporary bar for a wedding at a venue not licensed for the sale of alcohol, or may wish to provide a temporary disco in premises licensed for the sale of alcohol but not for the provision of regulated entertainment. For personal licence holders, the number of occasions which could be covered by these arrangements in any one year would be subject to a limit of 50.
- where **an individual who does not hold a personal licence** wishes to carry out one or more licensable activities at any premises, regardless of whether they are covered by a premises licence relating to those activities. For example, an individual may wish to run a bar and provide a band at a party to celebrate a 50th wedding anniversary. This may be done by the same person on no more than five occasions in any one calendar year.

In both cases, the arrangements would only apply where the number of attendees at the event is lower than 500. In addition, no premises may be used more than 12 times in any one calendar year by virtue of this Part, with an overall maximum of 15 days in any one year on which temporary events may take place at any particular premises.

*Section 98 – **Meaning of 'permitted temporary activity'***

165. This section provides that a 'permitted temporary activity' is one that is carried on in accordance with a temporary event notice given to the relevant licensing authority (see section 99 paragraph 166 below) and which satisfies the following conditions:

a) the temporary event notice has been duly acknowledged by the licensing authority (see section 102, paragraph 172 below) and notified to the police (see section 104, paragraph 174 below)

b) the temporary event notice has not been subsequently withdrawn by the individual giving the notice and

c) the licensing authority has not issued a counter-notice. A counter-notice would be issued, if necessary, following a hearing of any objections raised by the police to the effect that the crime prevention objective would be undermined by allowing the activity to go ahead (see section 105, paragraph 175 below) or if the permitted limits attaching to the person giving the notice or the premises would be exceeded (see section 107, paragraph 177 below)

*Section 99– **The relevant licensing authority***

166. This section defines the licensing authority for the purposes of this Part and as a consequence determines the authority, or authorities if the premises straddles more than one licensing authority area, to which a temporary event notice must be given.

*Section 100 – **Temporary event notice***

167. This section provides that an individual, known as a premises user, who proposes to carry on a licensable activity for a temporary period of not more than 96 hours may submit a notice to the relevant licensing authority of the proposal for the event. Such notice is defined as a temporary event notice. The premises user must be at least 18 years old.

168. Subsections (4) and (5) provide that the notice must be in a form prescribed in regulations by the Secretary of State and set out certain details about the proposed event:

a) the licensable activities that are to be carried out

b) the total length of the event – which must not exceed 96 hours

c) the times during the event that the licensable activities are to be carried out (for example, where an individual wishes to organise an event that covers 36 hours and where the bar will be open for two evenings within that time).

d) the maximum number of people to be allowed on to the premises at any one time – which must be less than 500

e) whether any alcohol sales are to be made for consumption on or off the premises (or both)

f) any other information that may be prescribed by regulations.

169. Subsection (6) requires that if the licensable activities proposed in the notice include the supply of alcohol, the notice must include a condition that all such supplies will be made by, or under the authority of, the premises user. The temporary event notice must be given to the licensing authority at least ten working days before the event. Before the time of the event the licensing authority must acknowledge the notice, the police must consider the notice and decide whether to give notice of objection and if the police object, the authority must, if necessary, convene a hearing, to decide whether to serve a counter notice. Although ten working days is the minimum specified, it is anticipated that in most circumstances greater notice will be given. The temporary event notice must be submitted in duplicate and accompanied by any fee prescribed in regulations made by the Secretary of State

170. Subsection (8) provides that the Secretary of State may by order (subject to affirmative resolution procedure) amend the limits as to the length of time permissible for any single

temporary event and the number of people who may attend an event. This will enable the Secretary of State to change the limits in response to experience of the working of the new regime.

Section 101 – ***Minimum of 24 hours between event periods***

171. This section provides that there must be a minimum period of 24 hours between temporary events held on the same premises by a premises user, or held by that user and another person who is related to, associated with or in business with that user. This prevents a premises user holding numerous consecutive temporary events as a means of avoiding an application for a premises licence. If a temporary event takes place on premises that are included within or include other premises where another temporary event takes place, then the two events are deemed to take place on the same premises.

Section 102 – ***Acknowledgement of notice***

172. Under this section, the licensing authority must acknowledge the temporary event notice given to it by a premises user by returning the duplicate notice to the premises user within a specified period. However, subsection (3) provides that an acknowledgement is not to be given if the licensing authority has already served a counter notice on the premises user under section 107 to the effect that the permitted number of events would be exceeded if the notified event took place.

Section 103– ***Withdrawal of notice***

173. This section provides that a premises user can withdraw a temporary event notice up to 24 hours before the event is scheduled to take place. Once withdrawn, the notice does not count towards the limits on the number of temporary event notices that may be submitted during a calendar year.

Section 104 – ***Objection to notice by police***

Section 105 - ***Counter notice following police objection and***

Section 106 - ***Modification of notice following police objection***

174. Section 104 provides that no later than ten working days before the beginning of the event period proposed in the temporary event notice, the premises user must give a copy of the notice to the chief officer of police in the relevant area. If the police are of the view that allowing the event to proceed would undermine the crime prevention objective, they must notify (an objection notice) the premises user and the relevant licensing authority, stating their reasons, no later than 48 hours after receipt of the copy of the notice.

175. Section 105 provides that, if the police object, the licensing authority must hold a hearing to consider the objection notice unless all parties agree that a hearing is unnecessary. If the authority accepts the police objection it must issue a counter-notice to the premises user in which case the event cannot proceed. If the authority does not accept the police objection it must inform the police. Any decision or counter-notice must be issued to the premises user at least 24 hours before the specified event period. A failure to do so will result in the premises user being able to proceed with the event.

176. Section 106 provides that, in cases where the police have given an objection notice, at any point between notification and the hearing the police and premises user may agree to modify the temporary event notice in order that it no longer undermines the promotion of the crime prevention objective. When temporary event notices are modified, the notice of objection by the police is withdrawn, and the modified temporary event notice has effect.

Section 107 - Counter notice where permitted limits exceeded

177. Subsection (1) requires a licensing authority to issue a counter-notice on receipt of a temporary event notice where

- the premises user is a personal licence holder who has already given 50 temporary event notices within the same calendar year as the specified event period, or
- when the premises user does not hold a personal licence, but has already given five temporary event notices in that year, or
- where twelve temporary event notices have been given in respect of the same premises in that year, or
- where temporary event notices are given for events at the same premises falling on more than 15 days in a year.

178. Subsection (12) gives the Secretary of State power by order to amend the limits in this section as to the numbers of temporary event notices that can be given by any person or in respect of any premises, or the number of days in any year when temporary events can take place at any premises. Again the orders are subject to the affirmative resolution procedure.

179. The effect of giving such a counter notice is that the proposed event is not a permitted temporary activity and is not authorised to proceed.

Section 108 – Right of entry where temporary event notice given and

Section 109 – Duty to keep and produce temporary event notice

180. Constables and officers of a licensing authority will be able to enter premises to assess the likely impact of a temporary event notice on the promotion of the crime prevention objective. The officer of a licensing authority must, if requested, produce evidence of his authority. It is an offence to obstruct such an officer exercising his powers under this section. It is already an offence to obstruct a constable in the exercise of his duty (see Police Act 1996).

181. The premises user must ensure that the notice is displayed at the premises or is kept there under his control or the control of a person nominated by him. In the latter case, a notice to that effect must be displayed at the premises. It is an offence for the premises user to fail to comply with this requirement. It is also an offence for a person who holds the premises licence under such arrangements to fail to produce it to a constable or an officer of a licensing authority when requested to do so.

Section 110 – Theft, loss etc. of temporary event notice

182. This section provides that premises users may apply to the licensing authority that acknowledged the temporary event notice for a copy of that notice if the notice has been lost, stolen, damaged or destroyed. If lost or stolen, the premises user is obliged to notify the police before a copy will be issued. There may be a fee prescribed for the issue of replacement documents. By virtue of subsection (2) an application for a copy of the notice cannot be made later than one month after the event. Subsection (6) provides that the copy of the notice will have effect as if it were the original.

PART 6: Personal Licences

183. Part 6 establishes a regime for the supply of alcohol to be regulated by the granting of personal licences to individuals. The licensing of individuals separately from the licensing of premises permits the movement of personal licence holders from one set of premises to another. The Act also provides the police and licensing authorities with powers to deal with errant personal licence holders.

184. The personal licence is to relate only to the supply of alcohol (as defined in section 111(2)) and not to other activities covered by the Act such as regulated entertainment or the provision of late night refreshment, for which no personal licence will be required. A personal licence does not authorise its holder to supply alcohol anywhere, but only from premises with a premises licence.

185. Where premises have a premises licence authorising the supply of alcohol, a personal licence must be held by the nominated individual responsible for the day-to-day running of the licensed premises, known as the designated premises supervisor. More than one individual at the licensed premises may hold a personal licence, although it will not be necessary for all staff to be licensed. But, all supplies of alcohol under a premises licence must be made by or under the authority of a personal licence holder.

186. A personal licence is issued for ten years in the first instance and there will be a presumption in favour of renewal if the licence holder has not been convicted of any offence.

187. The initial grant of a personal licence will additionally be subject to the possession of an accredited qualification. However, during the transitional period, existing holders of justices' licences for the sale of alcohol, will not be required to obtain an accredited qualification (see paragraph 23 of Schedule 8). Rather, there will be a general presumption that a personal licence will be granted automatically, except in limited circumstance (for example following representations by the police that to do so would undermine the crime prevention objective).

188. Convictions for offences which are relevant for the purposes of the determination of applications for the grant or renewal of a personal licence include:

- those involving serious crime
- those involving serious dishonesty
- those involving the supply of drugs
- certain sexual offences
- offences created by the Act.

(see paragraph 191 below on section 113 and Schedule 4).

Section 111 – ***Personal licence***

189. For the purposes of the Act, this section defines a personal licence as a licence granted by a licensing authority and permitting an individual to sell alcohol by retail or to supply alcohol by or on behalf of a club (in the latter case this would relate only to a supply authorised under a premises licence).

Section 112 – ***The relevant licensing authority***

190. This section provides that the relevant licensing authority in relation to a personal licence is the authority which originally granted the licence. The effect of this is that if a personal licence holder works in or moves to the area of a different licensing authority, the relevant licensing authority for the purpose of renewals etc will be unchanged.

Section 113 – ***Meaning of "relevant offence" and "foreign offence"***

191. For the purposes of Part 6 of the Act, relevant offences are defined as offences listed in Schedule 4. In subsection (2) the Secretary of State is given a power (subject to the negative resolution procedure) to amend that list. Subsection (3) provides that for the purposes of Part 6 of the Act, a 'foreign offence' is defined as an offence (other than a relevant offence) under the law of anywhere outside England and Wales. The significance of designation as a 'relevant offence' is that a conviction for such an

offence (or a comparable foreign offence), unless spent, must be taken into account by a licensing authority in its consideration of an application for the grant or renewal of a personal licence (see sections 120 and 121). If an existing personal licence holder is convicted of a relevant offence, his licence may be forfeited or suspended (see section 129).

*Section 114 – **Spent convictions***

192. This clause provides that convictions for relevant or foreign offences must be disregarded when spent under the Rehabilitation of Offenders Act 1974 for the purposes of Part 6 of the Bill.

*Section 115 – **Period of validity of personal licence and***

*Section 116 – **Surrender of personal licence***

193. Section 115 provides that a personal licence is valid for 10 years unless before then it is surrendered by the holder, revoked by the licensing authority or forfeited or suspended by the court. At the end of the 10 year period, the holder may apply for renewal to the licensing authority which issued the original licence and the authority can renew the licence for a further ten years or refuse the application for renewal. Licences do not have effect during periods of suspension. In some circumstances, a licence may extend beyond 10 years, pending a renewal or disposal of an appeal; for example, where an application for renewal of a personal licence has not been determined prior to the expiry of the 10 year validity period (see section 119). Section 116 provides that a personal licence holder may surrender his licence and sets out the procedural requirements of such a surrender.

*Section 117 – **Application for grant or renewal of personal licence***

*Section 118 – **Individual permitted to hold only one personal licence***

*Section 119 – **Licence continued pending renewal***

194. These sections set out the steps an individual must take to apply for the grant or renewal of a personal licence. An application for the grant of a personal licence must be made, ordinarily, to the authority for the area in which the applicant is normally resident. Applications for renewal are to be made to the licensing authority which originally granted the licence.

195. All applications must be made in the prescribed form and accompanied by the prescribed fee, information and documents. Applications for renewal can only be lodged within a two-month period beginning three months before the licence's expiry. If the licence expires before the application for renewal has been determined by the licensing authority, the licence remains in effect until a decision is made.

196. Only one licence can be held by a single individual at any one time.

*Section 120 – **Determination of application for grant***

197. This section prescribes the manner in which a licensing authority must determine an application for a personal licence. The criteria for the grant of a licence are that:

- the applicant is at least 18 years old
- he possesses an accredited licensing qualification or is of a prescribed description (see paragraph 200)
- he has not had a personal licence forfeited in the previous five years

- he has not been convicted of any relevant offences (see Schedule 4) or foreign offences (see paragraph 191)

198. Subsections (3) to (6) provide that the licensing authority must reject the application for a personal licence if the applicant fails to meet one of the first three eligibility criteria. If these are met but the applicant has been convicted of a relevant offence or a foreign offence, the licensing authority may grant the personal licence only after consulting the police. The chief officer of police must have regard to the conviction for any relevant offence, or for any foreign offence which he considers comparable to a relevant offence. Within 14 days of being notified, the chief officer must give to the licensing authority notice of objection to the grant of a licence if he is satisfied that granting the licence would undermine the prevention of crime and disorder (referred to here as "the crime prevention objective"). In the absence of such an objection, the licensing authority must grant the application.

199. When an objection is lodged by the police, the licensing authority must hold a hearing to decide whether to reject or grant the licence, and must give reasons for its decision. The need for a hearing may be dispensed with by agreement of the authority, the applicant and the police.

200. For the purpose of this section, the 'licensing qualification' must be recognised by the Secretary of State (by administrative action) or must be an equivalent qualification obtained in Scotland, Northern Ireland or an EEA state other than the UK.

Section 121 – ***Determination of application for renewal***

201. The licensing authority must renew a personal licence except where the applicant has been convicted of one or more relevant offences since the original grant of the licence or its last renewal. If such a conviction has occurred, the licensing authority must consult with the police and give them the opportunity to object to the renewal of the personal licence where they are satisfied that renewal would undermine the crime prevention objective. Where there is no objection the renewal must be granted. If the police object, a hearing must be held (unless the licence holder, the police and the licensing authority agree that this is unnecessary) and the authority must give the reasons for its decision.

Section 122 – ***Notification of determinations***

202. This section requires the licensing authority to notify the applicant and relevant chief officer of police of any decision to grant an application, explaining the decision in cases where an objection notice was given by the police. Notice of decisions to reject applications and the reasons for the decision must be given to applicants and the police.

Section 123 – ***Duty to notify licensing authority of convictions during application period***

203. Applicants convicted of a relevant offence or foreign offence (see section 113) in the period between an application being made and its determination (or withdrawal) must notify the relevant licensing authority of the conviction as soon as possible. Failure to do so is an offence.

Section 124 – ***Convictions coming to light after grant or renewal***

204. This section applies where an applicant for the grant or renewal of a personal licence is convicted of a relevant offence in the period between the application being made and its determination but knowledge of the conviction emerges only after the licence has been granted or renewed. The licensing authority may revoke a personal licence, after consultation with the police.

205. The section requires the licensing authority to consult the police on becoming aware of such a conviction. The police will then have the opportunity to give the licensing

authority notice that they object to the continuation of a licence where they believe that that would undermine the crime prevention objective. If the police object, a hearing must be held by the licensing authority (unless the licence holder, the police and the licensing authority agree that this is unnecessary). The licensing authority must give the reasons for its decision to the offender and to the police. A decision under this section does not have effect pending an appeal.

*Section 125 – **Form of personal licence***

206. This section makes provision for a personal licence to be in a prescribed form and lists the basic requirements as to the content of a licence, including a record of any convictions for relevant or foreign offences.

*Section 126 – **Theft, loss, etc. of personal licence***

207. Personal licence holders will be able to apply to the licensing authority that issued the licence for a copy if the licence has been lost, stolen, damaged or destroyed. If lost or stolen, this must be reported to the police before a copy will be issued. There may be a fee prescribed for the issue of replacement documents. The Act applies to a copy in the same way as it applies to the original.

*Section 127 – **Duty to notify change of name or address***

208. This section provides that the holder of a personal licence must notify the licensing authority of any change of name or address. Failure to do so is an offence.

*Section 128 – **Duty to notify court of personal licence***

*Section 129 – **Forfeiture or suspension of licence on conviction for relevant offence***

209. Where the holder of a personal licence is charged with a relevant offence, he must produce the licence to the court before the case against him is first heard in court (or if that is not possible, he must explain why). If an individual is granted a personal licence after being charged, he must produce the licence to the court (or explain why he cannot). A licence holder must also notify the court if, after having first produced his licence, the licence is renewed, surrendered or revoked. Failure to comply with any of these requirements is an offence.

210. Upon conviction of a personal licence holder of a relevant offence, the court may forfeit the personal licence or suspend it for up to 6 months. An order to forfeit or suspend the licence may itself be suspended by the convicting court allowing the licence to continue in force pending an appeal.

*Section 130 – **Powers of appellate court to suspend order under** section 129*

211. Orders made under section 129 may be suspended by the court on an appeal or an application for leave to appeal or an application for a quashing order by a defendant, allowing him to continue trading, if appropriate, while the appeal is being considered. If the court suspends the order it must notify the relevant licensing authority of that fact.

*Section 131 – **Court's duty to notify licensing authority of convictions***

212. This clause sets out the obligations of the court to the relevant licensing authority where a personal licence holder is convicted of a relevant offence. An appropriate officer of the court (defined in subsection (5)) must notify the relevant licensing authority of:

- the licence holder's name and address
- the nature and date of the conviction
- details of any sentence passed.

213. Where a conviction is quashed or a sentence altered on appeal, or where the Court of Appeal takes action in relation to a sentence it regards as unduly lenient, the court concerned must notify the relevant licensing authority.

*Section 132 – **Licence holder's duty to notify licensing authority of convictions***

214. This section requires that, where the holder of a licence is convicted of a relevant offence or foreign offence, and the courts are not aware of the existence of the licence, the holder must notify the licensing authority as soon as possible about the conviction and the outcome of any appeal against a conviction. Failure to comply with this section is an offence.

*Section 133 –**Form etc. of applications and notices under** Part 6*

215. This section allows for the detail of the form, manner and content of applications, and any accompanying documents or fees, to be set out in regulations.

*Section 134 – **Licensing authority's duty to update licence document***

216. Where certain changes have been made to the terms or effect of a personal licence, (for example, where it has been renewed, or a change of details has been notified), the licensing authority must make the necessary amendments to the licence.

217. The licensing authority may require the personal licence holder to present the licence for amendment. Failure by the licence holder to comply with this obligation, without reasonable excuse, is an offence.

*Section 135 – **Licence holder's duty to produce licence***

218. This section applies where the holder of a personal licence is on premises to sell, or authorise the sale of, alcohol by virtue of a premises licence or temporary event notice. A constable or officer of the licensing authority may require the holder to produce his personal licence. Failure to produce it is an offence.

PART 7: Offences

*Section 136 – **Unauthorised licensable activities***

219. This section makes it an offence to carry on or attempt to carry on a licensable activity without the authorisation provided by, as appropriate, a premises licence, a club premises certificate or a temporary event notice. It is also an offence knowingly to allow such an activity to be carried on. This provision is central to the enforcement of the licensing regime introduced by the Act.

220. Certain activities which would otherwise fall within the definition of "licensable activities" in section 1(1) are excluded from that definition by sections 173 to 175. Subsection (2) provides that an offence is not committed under section 136 if the only involvement of a person in the provision of regulated entertainment is his performance etc.

*Section 137 – **Exposing alcohol for unauthorised sale***

221. This section makes it an offence to expose alcohol for sale by retail (see the definition in section 192) in circumstances where the sale would not be under and in accordance with a premises licence, club premises certificate or temporary event notice. The effect of this provision is that an offence can be committed in a case where no sale or attempted sale is in fact made. Subsection (4) provides that a court which convicts a person of this offence may order the confiscation of the alcohol in question and its containers, which may then be either destroyed or dealt with as the court orders.

Section 138 – ***Keeping alcohol on premises for unauthorised sale***

222. This section makes it an offence to keep alcohol on premises with the intention of selling it by retail (see the definition in section 192) or supplying it (by or on behalf of a club or to the order of a member of the club) unless that sale or supply would be under and in accordance with an authorisation. Subsection (5) provides that a court which convicts a person of this offence may order the confiscation of the alcohol in question and its containers, which may then be either destroyed or dealt with as the court orders.

Section 139 - ***Defence of due diligence***

223. This section provides that a person who is charged with the offence of carrying on an unauthorised licensable activity, exposing alcohol for unauthorised sale or keeping alcohol in premises for unauthorised sale or supply has a defence if his act or omission was mistaken, was due to his relying on information given to him, was the fault of another person or was due to some cause beyond his control, and he took all reasonable precautions and exercised all due diligence to avoid committing the offence.

Section 140 – ***Allowing disorderly conduct on licensed premises etc.***

224. This section makes it an offence knowingly to allow disorderly conduct on licensed premises and thus re-enacts part of the existing offences in sections 172(1) and 172A(1) of the Licensing Act 1964. Subsection (2) of this section sets out the categories of person who may commit the offence. These include any person who works at the premises in a capacity that gives him the authority to prevent the conduct, a premises licence holder or designated premises supervisor, an officer or member of a club who is present at the time of the disorder and who has authority to prevent it, and a premises user (see the definition in section 100 (2)) who has given a temporary event notice in respect of those premises.

Section 141 – ***Sale of alcohol to a person who is drunk***

225. This section makes it an offence to sell or attempt to sell alcohol to a person who is drunk, or to allow alcohol to be sold to such a person, on relevant premises (see the definition in section 159). The section thus effectively re-enacts the existing offences in sections 172(3) and 172A(3) of the Licensing Act 1964. Subsection (2) of this section sets out the categories of person who may commit the offence. These include any person who works at the premises in a capacity that gives him the authority to sell the alcohol, a premises licence holder or designated premises supervisor, an officer or member of a club who is present at the time of the sale and who has authority to prevent it, and a premises user (see the definition in section 100(2)) who has given a temporary event notice in respect of those premises. Subsection (3) provides that the offence also covers supplies of alcohol by or on behalf of a club to or to the order of a member of the club.

Section 142 – ***Obtaining alcohol for a person who is drunk***

226. This section makes it an offence knowingly to obtain or attempt to obtain alcohol for consumption on relevant premises (see the definition in section 159) by a person who is drunk. The section thus effectively re-enacts the existing offence in section 173(1) of the Licensing Act 1964.

Section 143– ***Failure to leave licensed premises etc.***

227. This section provides that a person who is drunk or disorderly commits an offence if he fails to leave relevant premises (see the definition in section 159) at the request of a police constable or a person listed in subsection (2), or if he enters (or tries to enter) such premises when asked not to by such a person. No offence will be committed if the person has a reasonable excuse, for example, if he is disabled or injured and so unable to leave the premises. The persons listed in subsection (2) are:

- any person who works at the premises in a capacity that gives him the authority to make that request,
- a premises licence holder or designated premises supervisor,
- an officer or member of a club who is present at the time of the sale and who has authority to make that request, and
- a premises user (see the definition in section 100(2)) who has given a temporary event notice in respect of those premises.

228. Subsection (4) provides that a police constable must help to expel drunk or disorderly individuals from relevant premises, or help to prevent them entering as the case may be, if requested to do so by anyone listed above. The section thus re-enacts the provisions of section 174 of the Licensing Act 1964 but unlike that section is not limited to premises with a licence for alcohol sales.

*Section 144 – **Keeping of smuggled goods***

229. This section provides that it is an offence knowingly to keep or allow to be kept, on relevant premises (see the definition in section 159), any unlawfully imported goods or goods on which duty has not been paid. Subsection (2) sets out the categories of person who may commit the offence. These are

- any person who works at the premises in a capacity that gives him the authority to prevent those goods from being kept on the premises,
- a premises licence holder or designated premises supervisor,
- an officer or member of a club who is present at the time when the goods are kept on the premises and who has authority to prevent them being so kept, and
- a premises user (see the definition in section 100(2)) who has given a temporary event notice in respect of those premises.

Subsection (4) provides that a court which convicts a person of this offence may order the confiscation of the goods in question and their containers, which may then be either destroyed or dealt with as the court orders.

*Section 145 – **Unaccompanied children prohibited from certain premises.***

230. By virtue of this section it is an offence to admit children under 16 to certain categories of relevant premises (see section 159) if they are not accompanied by an adult and those premises are open for the supply of alcohol for consumption there. Those premises are

a) those exclusively or primarily used for the supply of alcohol for consumption on the premises, or

b) those open for the purposes of being used for the supply of alcohol for consumption on the premises by virtue of Part 5 (permitted temporary activities) and, at the time the temporary event notice in question has effect, they are exclusively or primarily used for such supplies.

It will also be an offence to allow an unaccompanied child under 16 to be on relevant premises at a time between the hours of midnight and 5 a.m when the premises are open for the supply for alcohol for consumption there.

231. Subsection (3) sets out the categories of persons who may commit the offence. These are:

- any person who works at the premises in a capacity that gives him the authority to request the child to leave,

- a premises licence holder or designated premises supervisor,
- an officer or member of a club who is present in a capacity which enables him to request the child to leave, and
- a premises user (see the definition in section 100(2)) who has given a temporary event notice in respect of those premises.

232. Subsection (6) provides for a defence where a person charged with an offence under this section believed the child was aged 16 or over, or the adult accompanying them was aged 18 or over, and either took all reasonable steps to establish the individual's age or nobody could reasonably have suspect from the individual's appearance that they were aged under 16 or 18. There is a further defence where someone is charged with an offence under this section because of the act or default of another person, and the person charged exercised all due diligence to avoid committing the offence. No offence is committed if the unaccompanied child is merely passing through the premises, where this is the only convenient route.

Section 146 – ***Sale of alcohol to children***

233. Existing legislation ties the offence of selling alcohol to children to licensed premises. This section makes it an offence to sell alcohol to children anywhere. Subsections (2) and (3) further provide that it is an offence for a club, or a person on behalf of a club, to supply alcohol to or to the order of a child who is a member of a club, or to any child on the order of a member of a club. Subsection (4) provides a defence if the seller believed that the purchaser was 18 or over and either he took all reasonable steps to establish the purchaser's age or nobody could reasonably have suspected from the purchaser's appearance that he was under 18. The second limb of that defence would cover a case where the purchaser who was under 18 looked exceptionally old for his age. The defendant will be deemed to have taken 'all reasonable steps' if he asked the individual for evidence of his age. However, if it is proved by the prosecution that the evidence of age was such that no reasonable person would have been convinced by it (for example if the proof of age was either an obvious forgery or clearly belonged to another person), the defence will fail. Subsection (6) provides a further defence in circumstances where the sale or supply was made by someone other than the person charged with the offence (for example, where the manager of a pub is charged with the offence although the actual sale was made by a barman) if the person charged exercised all due diligence to avoid committing the offence.

Section 147 – ***Allowing sale of alcohol to children***

234. This section provides that it is an offence knowingly to allow the sale (or in, the case of clubs, the supply) of alcohol to a child, on relevant premises (see the definition in section 159). Subsections (2) and (4) set out the categories of person who may commit the offence. These include any person who works at the premises in a capacity that gives him the authority to prevent the sale (or supply), and, in the case of a supply by or on behalf of a club, an officer or member of the club who is present at the time of the supply in a capacity that gives him authority to prevent that supply.

Section 148 – ***Sale of liqueur confectionery to children under 16***

235. This section makes it an offence to sell liqueur confectionery – as defined in section 191(2) – to a child under 16, or for a club or person on behalf of a club to supply it to or to the order of such a child. Subsection (3) provides a defence if the seller believed that the purchaser was 16 or over and if either he took all reasonable steps to establish the purchaser's age or if nobody could reasonably have suspected from the purchaser's appearance that he was under 16. The defendant will be deemed to have taken 'all reasonable steps' if he asked the individual for evidence of his age, and that evidence was such that it would have convinced a reasonable person. Subsection

(5) provides a further defence in circumstances where the sale or supply was made by someone other than the person charged with the offence, if the person charged exercised all due diligence to avoid committing the offence.

*Section 149 – **Purchase of alcohol by or on behalf of children***

236. Subsection (1) makes it an offence for a child to buy or attempt to buy alcohol whether or not on licensed premises, or, if he is a member of a club, for him to have alcohol supplied to him by the club (in circumstances where he actively caused the supply) or attempt to do so. The offence will not be committed if the child was asked by a police constable or trading standards officer, acting in the course of their duty, to buy or attempt to buy alcohol in order to conduct test purchasing operations to establish whether licensees and staff working in licensed premises are complying with the prohibition on underage sales.

237. Subsection (3) makes it an offence for a person to act as an agent for a child in purchasing or attempting to purchase alcohol, for example, if a child gives money to an adult to buy alcohol in an off-licence for consumption by the child. The offence also applies where a member of a club has alcohol supplied to a child or attempts to do so. Subsection (4) makes it a further offence for a person to buy or attempt to buy alcohol for consumption by a child on licensed premises, for example, where a father buys a drink for his son in a pub. The offence also applies where a member of a club has alcohol supplied to a child (in circumstances where he actively caused the supply) or attempts to do so. Subsection (5) provides that this offence will not be committed if a person aged 18 or over buys beer, wine or cider for a person aged 16 or 17 to consume with a table meal on relevant premises (see the definitions in section 159), in circumstances where the 16 or 17 year old is accompanied by an adult. This provision thus re-enacts the existing exemption in section 169D of the Licensing Act 1964.

*Section 150 – **Consumption of alcohol by children***

238. Subsection (1) makes it an offence for a child knowingly to consume alcohol on relevant premises (see the definition in section 159). The offence will thus not be committed if the child inadvertently consumes the alcohol, for example if his drink is spiked. Subsection (2) also makes it an offence knowingly to allow the consumption of alcohol by a child on relevant premises. Subsection (3) sets out the categories of person who may commit this offence. These include any person who works at the premises in a capacity that gives him the authority to prevent the consumption and, in the case of a supply by a club, to any officer or member of a club who is present at the time of the consumption in a capacity which allows him to prevent it. Subsection (4) provides that the offences in this section will not be committed where a 16 or 17-year-old consumes beer, wine or cider with a table meal (see the definition in section 159) in circumstances where he is accompanied by an adult.

*Section 151 – **Delivering alcohol to children***

239. This section sets out offences relating to the delivery of alcohol to children. Subsection (1) provides that it is an offence for someone working on relevant premises (see the definition in section 159) knowingly to deliver to a child alcohol which is sold on the premises or supplied there by or on behalf of a club. The offence would cover, for example, circumstances where a child takes delivery of a consignment of alcohol bought by his father from an off-licence (in a case where the exceptions mentioned below do not apply). Subsections (2) and (3) provide that it is also an offence for a person working on relevant premises and in a position which gives him authority to prevent it knowingly to allow another person to deliver alcohol to children. This offence would cover, for example, a person who authorises a delivery of the sort mentioned above. Subsections (4) and (5) provide that this offence will also apply in the case of a delivery by or on behalf of a club or to or to the order of a member of the club, where the delivery is

allowed by a person working on the premises in a capacity which gives him authority to prevent it.

240. Subsection (6) provides that the offences in this section are not committed if the alcohol is delivered to the home or place of work of the purchaser or person who is supplied (for example, where a child answers the door and signs for the delivery of his father's order at his house), nor where the job of the minor who took delivery of the alcohol involves delivery of alcohol (for example, where a 16 year old office worker is sent to collect a delivery for his employer), nor where the alcohol is sold or supplied for consumption on the relevant premises.

*Section 152 – **Sending a child to obtain alcohol***

241. This section re-enacts the existing offence (in section 169G of the Licensing Act 1964) of knowingly sending a child to obtain alcohol which is sold for consumption off the premises, or which is supplied by or on behalf of a club to or to the order of a member of the club for such consumption. This offence would cover, for example, circumstances where a parent sends their child to an off-licence to collect some alcohol which had been bought over the telephone. Subsection (2) provides that the offence will be committed regardless of whether the child is sent to the actual premises from where the alcohol is sold or supplied, or whether he is sent to other premises to which the alcohol has been sent. Subsection (3) provides that the offence will not be committed where the minor's works at the premises in question and his job involves taking deliveries of alcohol. Subsection (4) provides that the offence will also not be committed if the child is sent by a police or trading standards officer, in the course of his duty, to obtain alcohol to test the compliance of the retailer with the prohibition on underage sales.

*Section 153 – **Prohibition of unsupervised sales by children***

242. This section re-enacts provisions in the Licensing Act 1964 so that it is an offence knowingly to allow an individual under the age of 18 to sell or, in the case of a club, to supply alcohol unless each such sale or supply has been specifically approved. Subsection (4) sets out the categories of person who may commit this offence. These are

- a premises licence holder, designated premises supervisor or someone over 18 authorised by them, or
- in the case of a club, any member of officer of the club who is present on the premises in a capacity that enables him to prevent the supply, or
- in a case where the premises are used for a temporary permitted activity, the premises user or a person over 18 authorised by him.

Subsection (2) provides that the offence in this section is not committed where the alcohol is sold for consumption with a table meal in a part of the premises used only for this purpose. The effect of this exception is that, for example, a minor will be able to serve alcohol in a restaurant.

*Section 154 – **Enforcement role for weights and measures authorities***

243. This provision re-enacts section 169I of the Licensing Act 1964 which confers on weights and measures authorities the role of conducting test purchase operations to check retailers' compliance with the prohibition on underage sales. In practice, these activities are usually carried out by trading standards officers. Subsection (2) provides that a weights and measures inspector may either make purchases himself or may authorise another person to do so. Thus, for example, he might lawfully ask a child to attempt to purchase alcohol.

Section 155 – Confiscation of sealed containers for alcohol

244. This section amends the Criminal Justice and Police Act 2001 and the Confiscation of Alcohol (Young Persons) Act 1997 so that the police have the power to confiscate alcohol in sealed containers from anyone in an area which has been designated by the local authority for the purposes of curbing anti-social behaviour and from people under 18 in any public place. Police powers in relation to confiscation of alcohol currently apply only in relation to opened containers.

Section 156 – Prohibition of sale of alcohol on moving vehicles

245. This section makes it an offence to sell alcohol by retail on or from any vehicle which is not permanently or temporarily parked. Subsection (3) provides a defence in circumstances where:

- the sale was mistaken, was due to the seller relying on information given to him, was the fault of another person or was due to some cause beyond his control, and
- he took all reasonable precautions and exercised all due diligence to avoid committing the offence.
- For example, a person might mistakenly believe the beverages he is serving are non-alcoholic.

Section 157 – Power to prohibit sale of alcohol on trains

246. Subsections (1) and (2) provide for the prohibition of sales of alcohol at specified stations or on trains travelling between specified stations for a specified period. A prohibition order may be made by local magistrates on the application of a police officer of at least the rank of inspector, if the magistrates are satisfied that the order is necessary for the prevention of disorder. Subsection (4) requires the police officer who applied for the order (or another police officer who has been designated by the chief officer of police) to serve a copy of the order on the train operator or operators concerned. It is to be an offence knowingly to sell alcohol, or to permit its sale, in contravention of such an order.

Section 158 – False statements made for the purposes of this Act

247. This section provides that it is an offence for a person knowingly or recklessly to make any false statement in connection with applications and notices under the Act.

Part 8: Closure of premises

General

248. Part 8 of the Act contains provisions empowering the courts and the police to make temporary closure orders in respect of certain premises.

249. It re-enacts with some modifications the provisions to be found in sections 179A to 179K and 188 of the Licensing Act 1964. In particular the provisions of the Act are not restricted to premises licensed for the sale of alcohol, but extend to all relevant premises (see section 161(8)).

Section 160 – Order to close premises in an area experiencing disorder

250. This section sets out the power to close all premises with a premises licence, or in respect of which a temporary event notice has effect, which are located in a particular geographical area for a period not exceeding 24 hours. The power is exercisable by a magistrates' court on application from a police officer of the rank of superintendent or above. It is exercisable only where the court thinks such an order is necessary to prevent disorder. It is an offence to keep open premises that are the subject of a closure

order. Section 171(2) and (3) make provision about when premises are "open" for these purposes.

*Section 161 – **Closure order for identified premises***

251. This section provides a senior police officer with the power to close specific premises for up to 24 hours. A closure order may be made upon two grounds, the first of which is where there is actual or likely disorder to the extent that the closure of the related premises is necessary in the interests of public safety. The second ground is where closure is necessary to prevent a public nuisance, owing to the noise emanating from the premises.

252. In deciding whether to make a closure order, the police officer must have regard to the conduct of certain defined individuals at the premises. The purpose of this provision is to allow discretion in cases where, for example, it is clear that those managing the premises are treating the disorder or disturbance with sufficient gravity and are taking steps to reduce it or bring it under control.

*Section 162 – **Extension of closure order***

253. This section empowers a senior police officer to extend, in certain limited circumstances, the period for which a closure order may have effect. Such an extension may be for a further period of 24 hours. More than one extension may be made.

*Section 163 – **Cancellation of closure order***

254. This section empowers a senior police officer to cancel a closure order at any time before it has been considered by a magistrates' court pursuant to the latter's power in section 165. Such a cancellation must be made where the officer does not reasonably believe that closure of the premises is necessary because of disorder, likely disorder or because of noise emanating from the premises. The officer must give notice to the licence holder, designated premises supervisor, premises user or manager of the premises where it is decided to cancel a closure order.

*Section 164 – **Application to magistrates' court by police***

255. After a closure order comes into force, the responsible senior police officer must apply to the magistrates' court as soon as possible to allow for the consideration of the order by the court. Notice of such an application and details of the order itself must also be given to the relevant licensing authority (as defined in section 171).

*Section 165 – **Consideration of closure order by magistrates' court***

256. The relevant magistrates' court to whom an application has been made under section 164 must hold a hearing. The court can take a number of courses of action in relation to the order, including revoking the closure order, or ordering its extension until the licensing authority has conducted a review of the order under section 167. The court may also make an order determining that the premises should be, or should remain, closed until such a review has been completed.

*Section 166 – **Appeal from decision of magistrates' court***

257. This section provides a right of appeal to the Crown Court against decisions made by a magistrates' court under section 165.

*Section 167 – **Review of premises licence following closure order***

258. Where a licensing authority has received notice from a magistrates' court pursuant to section 165 (consideration of closure order by magistrates' court), in respect of a closure

order for identified premises having effect in relation to premises, it must review any premises licence having effect in respect of those premises.

259. The licensing authority may take steps to further the licensing objectives including revocation of the licence, modification of the licence conditions, the exclusion of certain licensable activities or the removal of the designated premises supervisor. For example, where the licensing authority determines that the lack of experience or expertise of the designated premises supervisor has contributed to the level of disorder that has given rise to a closure order, it may specify that the individual concerned should be removed from that position. Similarly, it may determine that imposing a condition on the licence to the effect that additional security staff should be employed would reduce disorder.

*Section 168 – **Provision about decisions under** section 167*

260. This section makes provision for premises subject to a closure order under section 161 (closure orders of identified premises) to remain closed during any appeal against the licensing authority's decision to revoke the premises licence (although the licence would remain in force). Under Schedule 5 a magistrates' court may order the re-opening of the premises pending the appeal.

*Section 171 – **Interpretation of** Part 8*

261. This section sets out various definitions for the purposes of this Part. The section explains in what circumstances premises will be treated as "open" and states that certain activities will not count for the purposes of determining whether premises are "open". These are –

- in a case where the premises do not have a premises licence, but have a temporary event notice, any activities (other than licensable activities) taking place outside the event period in the notice
- any use for qualifying club activities under a club premises certificate
- any supplies of hot food and drink which are not licensable activities by reason of their being supplied to members of a club or the guests of members

Part 9: **Miscellaneous and Supplementary**

General

262. This Part of the Act covers a number of miscellaneous issues.

*Section 172 – **Relaxation of opening hours for special occasions***

263. The Secretary of State may make an order to provide for premises with a premises licence or club premises certificate to open for specified, generally extended, hours on special occasions – for example, Royal Jubilees.

*Section 173 – **Activities in certain locations not licensable***

264. This section provides that activities which would otherwise be "licensable activities" for the purposes of the Act are not such activities if carried on in certain places (e.g. aboard a vessel on an international journey).

265. The "examination station" of a designated airport (as mentioned in subsection (1)) is essentially that part of the airport beyond the security check-in.

*Section 174 – **Certifying premises on grounds of national security***

266. Ministers of Cabinet rank, or the Attorney General, may grant a certificate in respect of any premises on the grounds of national security. The effect of the certificate is that

activities carried on at the premises are not "licensable activities" for the purposes of the Act (see section 173(1)(g)). This power may be used in circumstances where the inspection of a particular premises, for purposes of the licensing regime, would give rise to a security risk.

*Section 175 – **Exemption for raffle, tombola etc.***

267. The giving of a sealed container of alcohol as a prize in a lottery will not be counted as a licensable activity for the purposes of the Act if:

- the lottery is promoted as incidental to a bazaar, sale of work, fete, dinner, dance, sporting or athletic events or other entertainment of a similar character
- after the deduction of all relevant expenses, none of the proceeds are used for private gain
- none of the prizes are money prizes
- the tickets or chances are sold or issued and the result of the draw is announced at the time of, and in the same place as, the entertainment
- the lottery or draw is not the main inducement to attend the entertainment

268. Subsection (3) defines the expenses which are 'relevant' for the purposes of this section as those incurred in the course of arranging and holding the entertainment, and those in connection with the lottery or draw, including the printing of tickets and buying prizes.

*Section 176 – **Prohibition of alcohol sales at service areas, garages etc.***

269. This section provides for a general prohibition on the sale of alcohol at motorway service areas and garage forecourts. The Secretary of State may by order exclude or include any descriptions of premises from the set of those to which the prohibition applies. An example of the possible use of this power would be to lift the prohibition from garages, perhaps in rural areas, where the turnover is made up of a specified proportion of non-petrol sales. But the power is not limited to premises related to motorway service areas and garages.

*Section 177 – **Dancing and live music in certain small premises***

270. This section provides that where

- a premises licence or club premises certificate authorises the sale of alcohol for consumption on the premises and the provision of "music entertainment" (live music or dancing),
- the relevant premises are used primarily for the consumption of alcohol on the premises, and
- the premises have a capacity limit of up to 200

any conditions relating to the provision of the music entertainment imposed on the licence by the licensing authority, other than those set out by the licence or certificate holder in his operating schedule, will be suspended except where they were imposed as being necessary for public safety or the prevention of crime and disorder.

271. In addition, where

- a premises licence or club premises certificate authorises the provision of music entertainment, and
- the premises have a capacity limit of 200

then, during the hours of 8am and midnight, if the premises are being used for the provision of live unamplified music but no other description of regulated entertainment any conditions imposed on the licence by the licence authority, again other than those set out in the operating schedule, which relate to the provision of the music entertainment will be suspended.

272. This section can be disapplied in relation to any condition of a premises licence or club premises certificate following a review of the licence or certificate.

*Section 178 – **Right of freeholder etc to be notified of licensing matters***

273. This section provides that a person with a property interest in any premises situated in the licensing authority's area may give notice of his interest to that authority in a prescribed form and on payment of a fee to be prescribed by the Secretary of State. Those who may take advantage of this arrangement include the freeholder or leaseholder, a legal mortgagee in respect of the premises, a person in occupation of the premises or any other person prescribed by the Secretary of State. The notice will have effect for 12 months but a new notice can be given every year. Whilst their notice has effect, the person or business involved will ,if any change relating to the premises concerned has been made to the licensing register which the licensing authority has a duty to keep under section 8, be notified of the matter to which the change relates.. They will also be notified of their right under section 8 to request a copy of the information contained in any entry in the register .

*Section 179 – **Rights of entry to investigate licensable activities***

274. This section provides for police officers or other authorised persons to enter premises to ensure that any licensable activities are being carried on under the appropriate authorisations. It is already an offence under the Police Act 1996 to obstruct a constable in the exercise of his duty. It will be an offence under the Act to obstruct other authorised persons in exercising this power.

*Section 180 - **Right of entry to investigate offences***

275. This section provides that police officers may enter and search premises where there is reason to believe an offence under the Act has been, is being or is about to be committed, and may use reasonable force to gain entry. It will be an offence intentionally to prevent the exercise of these powers.

*Section 181 – **Appeals against decisions of licensing authorities***

276. Applicants for and holders of licences and club premises certificates, applicants for provisional notices and interim authority notices and applicants for temporary event notices, responsible authorities and interested parties all have rights of appeal to a magistrates' court against decisions of a licensing authority. The appeals mechanism is set out at Schedule 5. This section sets out the powers of the magistrates in determining such appeals.

*Section 182- **Guidance***

277. The Act provides that licensing authorities must have regard to guidance issued by the Secretary of State in formulating their framework policy documents and in discharging their other functions under the Act. This section provides for the issue and revision of this guidance and its publication and requires the Secretary of State in the case of the initial guidance to issue it only after it has been approved in draft form by resolution of each House of Parliament. Revisions of the guidance come into force when laid before Parliament. However, they can be prayed against within 40 days and if disapproved a further revision would have to be laid under the same procedure. In the meantime the revised guidance retains full force and effect pending the laying of the further revision.

Section 183 - ***Hearings***

278. Procedures for hearings will be prescribed in regulations, which may require authorities to notify certain persons of hearings, ensure the expedition of urgent cases and set out rules relating to evidence and legal representation and the period within which steps must be taken. Licensing authorities may not make any orders as to the costs of hearings under the Act.

Section 184 – ***Giving of notices, etc.***

279. This section sets out rules for delivery of documents to the licensing authority and any other person or body affected by the licensing regime.

Section 185 – ***Provision of information***

280. This section provides for the sharing of information by licensing authorities and responsible authorities for the purposes of the Act.

Section 186 - ***Proceedings for offences***

281. This section sets out the bodies that can bring a prosecution for an offence contained in the Act. It also extends the limitation period for bringing summary proceedings from the usual period of six months to a period of 12 months.

Section 187 – ***Offences by bodies corporate etc.***

282. This section provides that where an offence under the Act is committed with the consent or connivance of a director, member of the management committee, chief executive, manager, secretary or similar officer of a corporate body (e.g. a limited company), or through attributable neglect, the officer as well as the corporate body commits the offence. In the case of partnerships, the consent, connivance or attributable neglect of a partner, or in the case of other unincorporated associations the consent or connivance of an officer of the association or member of its governing body, would make the individual and the organisation guilty of the offence.

Section 188 – ***Jurisdiction and procedure in respect of offences***

283. This section provides that any fine imposed following the conviction of an unincorporated association should be paid out of the association's funds. It provides that any proceedings brought against unincorporated associations must be brought in the name of the association, and not the name of any of its members. Certain legal procedures and rules relating to the service of documents will apply to unincorporated associations as to bodies corporate.

Section 189 - ***Vessels, vehicles and moveable structures***

284. The provisions for premises licences, club certificates and temporary permissions will apply to a vessel not permanently moored or berthed in a particular place as though they were premises situated at the place where it is normally moored or berthed. A vehicle or moveable structure – e.g. tent or inflatable building – which is not permanently located in the same place will be treated as premises located at any place where it is parked or set. So if licensable activities are carried on or from the vehicle when it is parked, a premises licence, club premises certificate or temporary event notice will be required, and where such activities take place when it is parked in more than one place, the vehicle will be treated as if it were separate premises at each location, and separate premises licence etc. will be required. Sections 29 to 31 (provisional statements re premises licences) do not apply to vessels, vehicles or moveable structures.

*Section 190 - **Location of sales***

285. Where the place where a sale of alcohol takes place is different from the place from which the alcohol is supplied, the sale is treated as having happened at the place from which the alcohol is appropriated to the contract. For example, when alcohol is bought via mail order or a telephone call centre, the sale will, for the purposes of the Act, have taken place at the warehouse from which the alcohol would be delivered, and not the call centre The requirement for a premises licence will therefore apply to the warehouse rather than the call centre.

*Section 191 – **Meaning of "alcohol"***

286. For the purpose of the Act, 'alcohol' means: spirits, wine, beer, cider or any other fermented, distilled or spirituous liquor. It does **not** include any liquor of 0.5% strength or below at the time of the sale or supply in question, perfume, flavouring essence, alcohol which is, or is included in, any medicine, denatured alcohol (methylated spirits) or alcohol contained in liqueur confectionery (as defined in subsection (2)).

*Section 192– **Meaning of 'sale by retail'***

287. This section defines 'sale by retail', of alcohol, for the purposes of the Act as a sale to a person other than a sale to a trader for trade purposes, to a club which holds a club premises certificate, to a premises licence holder or to a premises user with a temporary event notice for purposes permitted by those certificates, licences or notices. The purpose of these exemptions is to ensure that purely "business to business" sales are excluded from the scope of the Act.

*Section 195 – **Crown application***

288. This section provides for the Act to apply to the Crown and to Crown property. It also applies to land of the Duchies of Lancaster and Cornwall (except to the extent that they are occupied by the Queen or the Prince of Wales).

289. The Board of the Green Cloth is a committee of the Royal Household responsible for licensing inns "within the verge of the Palace" (i.e. Buckingham Palace). There are a number of public houses within the jurisdiction of the Board, which is limited to what used to be the private grounds of the Sovereign, and includes Carlton House Terrace, the northern end of Whitehall and the National Gallery (the former Royal Stables). Those areas currently within the jurisdiction of the Board of Green Cloth are within the remit of the Act, so that licensing functions in respect of these areas are to be carried out by the relevant licensing authority.

290. Activities carried out at royal palaces are not "licensable activities" for the purposes of the Act (see section 173). This would include, for example, the Palace of Westminster.

*Section 196 – **Removal of privileges and exemptions***

291. Under the Licensing Act 1964, the historical exemptions and privileges enjoyed by the University of Cambridge and the Honourable Company of Vintners were preserved and so the licensing requirements did not apply to either of them. The new regime applies across the board and this section makes it clear that none of those privileges or exemptions are being preserved.

*Section 197 - **Regulations and orders***

292. Most secondary legislation made under the Act is to be subject to the negative resolution procedure. But the following secondary legislation is to be subject to the affirmative procedure:

a) an order under section 100(8) (alteration of maximum temporary event period etc.)

b) an order under section 107(12) (alteration on limit on number of temporary event notices)

c) an order under section 172 (relaxation of opening hours for special occasions);

d) an order under section 176(3) (order amending definition of "excluded premises" where alcohol sales are prohibited);

e) order under paragraph 4 of Schedule 1 (amendments to the meaning of "regulated entertainment").

293. Commencement orders and the order prescribing the start of the first period for which licensing authorities must prepare a statement of licensing policy (see section 5) will be subject to neither procedure. Regulations or an order under the Act may make transitional provisions.

Section 198 – ***Minor and consequential amendments***

294. This section gives effect to Schedule 6, which sets out minor and consequential amendments to existing legislation required by the Act. The Secretary of State has a limited power to make consequential amendments by order. He may only make amendments, consequential on any provision of the Act, to any Act or subordinate legislation made before the provision in question comes into force.

Section 199 – ***Repeals***

295. This section gives effect to Schedule 7, which sets out the existing legislation repealed by the Act, and the extent of any repeal.

Section 200 – ***Transitional provisions etc.***

296. This section gives effect to Schedule 8, which sets out the transitional and transitory provisions.

Section 201 – ***Short title, commencement and extent***

297. The Act extends to England and Wales. And the amendment of the Confiscation of Alcohol (Young Persons) Act 1997 (see section 155) extends also to Northern Ireland.

Schedule 1 – ***Provision of regulated entertainment***

298. This Schedule defines the provision of regulated entertainment as covering entertainment provided solely or partly for members of the public, or exclusively to club members and their guests, or for which a charge is made, which is provided for profit (which will include to raise money for charity). It also covers the provision of entertainment facilities for participating in entertainment.

299. The definition would cover entertainment staged by a charity for purposes of fundraising, but would not, for example, include the provision of entertainment for a company or firm for its clients, for which no charge was made but which was connected with stimulating general goodwill which might be advantageous for the business.

300. Forms of entertainment to be regulated by the Act include:

a) **plays** – both performance and rehearsal;

b) **the showing of films** (or any exhibition of moving pictures);

c) **all indoor sporting events**. For the purposes of the Act, an indoor sporting event is one which takes place inside a building for spectators wholly inside that building. A sporting event that takes place at a venue whose roof can be opened or closed would not constitute an indoor event, even when the roof is closed. For the purposes of this Act, sport is defined as any contest in which physical skill is the main factor and any form of physical recreation engaged in for the purposes of competition or display. For example, tennis would be covered by the definition. However, a game of chess contested publicly would not;

d) **outdoor boxing and wrestling matches**. No other form of outdoor sport would be regulated by the Act;

e) **music**: both the performance of live music and the playing of recorded music. No distinction is made in the Act between different musical styles; and

f) performance of **dance**;

where the entertainment takes place in the presence of an audience and is provided for their entertainment.

301. The Secretary of State may by order (subject to the affirmative resolution procedure) amend the definitions included in the Schedule.

302. A number of exemptions to regulated entertainment are included in the Act including:-

a) the showing to an audience of television and radio programmes forming part of a programme service within the meaning of the Broadcasting Act 1990 (so long as the programmes have not been pre-recorded)

b) music which is incidental to an activity which is not itself the provision of regulated entertainment, for example, music played in lifts or piano music played in the background in a restaurant.

c) film exhibitions used for product demonstration, advertisement, information, education or instruction. This would exempt, for example, educational films shown in schools, or special advertisements shown at product display stands in shopping centres.

d) the provision of entertainment or entertainment facilities for the purposes of, or incidental to, a religious meeting or service or provided at a place of public religious worship. This would exempt, not only the singing of hymns or other religious material at a religious service, but also the performance of a classical concert at a church.

e) entertainment at a garden fete.

f) morris dancing, or dancing of a similar nature.

g) entertainment provided on vehicles in motion.

*Schedule 2 – **Provision of late night refreshment***

303. For the purposes of the Act, late night refreshment means the supply of hot food or hot drink to the public, for consumption on or off the premises, between 11pm and 5am. It also means the supply of hot food or hot drink between those hours on premises to which the public has access. The Schedule contains a definition of "hot" for the purposes of the Act.

304. Certain supplies are not covered by the definition of late night refreshment, including:

a) supply to guests of hotels or similar premises, e.g. guest houses, lodging houses, caravan or camping sites or other premises supplying accommodation as their main purpose

b) supply to members of recognised clubs

c) supply to employees of a particular employer – for example, where refreshment is made available to employees whose shift patterns require them to be present at the workplace between 11pm and 5am

d) premises already licensed under certain other Acts – for instance those used as "near beer" premises in London (where certain descriptions of non-alcoholic beverages are sold).

There are specific exemptions for the provision of hot food or drink by vending machines (where the money is inserted by members of the public rather than the staff at the premises), food or drink supplied free of charge, or by a registered charity.

Schedule 3 – Matters to be entered in licensing register

305. This Schedule sets out the information to be recorded in the licensing register that all licensing authorities will be obliged to maintain (see section 8).

Schedule 4 – Personal licence: relevant offences

306. This Schedule lists those offences that could, on conviction, rule out the grant or renewal of a personal licence to the individual convicted, or lead to revocation of an existing licence held by a licence holder so convicted.

Schedule 5 – Appeals

307. This Schedule provides for decisions made by a licensing authority to be subject to appeal to a magistrates' court by any party involved in the decision – applicants, responsible authorities and interested parties. So, an applicant for a premises licence may appeal to the magistrates' court against the inclusion in the licence by the licensing authority of conditions that the applicant sees as unreasonably restrictive. At the same time, the police, for example, or a local resident would have a right of appeal against conditions that appeared to them to fail to promote the licensing objectives.

308. Part 1 of this Schedule sets out the appeals process with regard to premises licences.

- Applicants may appeal to the magistrates court if the licensing authority has rejected their application for a premises licence, for a variation of a premises licence, for the variation of a designated premises supervisor or for a transfer of a licence.
- If a licence is granted, the licence holder may appeal against the imposition of conditions on that licence, the exclusion of a licensable activity or refusal to specify an individual as supervisor.
- Those who made relevant representations during the course of an application may appeal against the decision to grant a licence.
- Applicants or any person who made a relevant representations may appeal against the decision to issue a provisional statement.
- Where a licensing authority takes the step of modifying the conditions of the licence before granting a variation, the applicant may appeal. Any person who made relevant representations can appeal against the decision to vary the licence.
- The chief officer of police who gave a notice may appeal against the grant of an application to specify an individual as a premises supervisor or against the decision to transfer a licence.
- Where a licensing authority decides to cancel an interim authority notice following a notice from the chief officer of police, the person who gave the interim authority notice may appeal against the decision. Where the licensing authority does not

cancel the interim authority notice following a notice from the police, the chief officer of police may appeal.

- The decision in relation to a review of a premises licence may be brought to appeal by the applicant for the review; the premises licence holder or any one who made relevant representations.

309. Part 2 sets out the appeals procedure in relation to club premises certificates.

- Clubs applying for a premises certificate or applying to vary a certificate may appeal against the decision by the licensing authority to reject the application.
- If a certificate is granted, the holding club may appeal against the imposition of conditions or the exclusion of a licensable activity.
- Those who made relevant representations during the course of an application may appeal against the decision to grant a certificate.
- Where a licensing authority takes the step of modifying the certificate before granting a variation, the club may appeal. Any person who made relevant representations can appeal against the decision to vary the certificate.
- The decision in relation to a review of a club premises certificate may be brought to appeal by the applicant for the review, the certificate-holding club or anyone who made relevant representations.

310. Part 3 of this Schedule covers appeals in relation to temporary event notices, personal licences and closure orders.

- In relation to temporary event notices, premises users may appeal against the decision by a licensing authority to give a counter notice.
- Applicants for personal licences may appeal against the decision to reject an application for or application to renew a licence. Where the police lodged an objection notice to the grant or renewal of a personal licensing, and the licensing authority grants or renews the licence, the police may appeal.
- Personal licence holders may appeal against revocation of that licence by the licensing authority. Where the police have given notice about relevant offences which come to light after the granting or renewal of a licence, and the licensing authority decide not to revoke the licence, the police may appeal against the decision.
- The licence holder or any person who made representations on a review of a premises licence following a closure order may appeal against the outcome of the review.

Schedule 6 – Minor and consequential amendments

311. This Schedule sets out the amendments to existing legislation required by the Act.

Schedule 7- Repeals

312. This Schedule sets out the existing legislation which will be repealed by the Act.

Schedule 8 – Transitional provision etc.

313. Part 1 of this Schedule sets out the transitional provisions for premises licences. A person who is either the holder of an existing licence or who has the consent of the holder of an existing licence may, within 6 months of a day appointed for the purposes of this Part of the Schedule, apply to the relevant licensing authority (determined in accordance with section 12 in Part 3 of the Act) for the conversion of an existing licence, or existing licences, to a premises licence. The Part lists, in paragraph 1(1), the existing

licences in the current licensing regimes which may be converted to a premises licence and defines existing licensable activities to mean licensable activities authorised under an existing licence and any other licensable activities which may be carried on at the premises to which the existing licence relates which may be carried on by virtue of the existence of the licence.

314. Paragraph 2(4) and (5) details the matters to be specified in an application for the conversion of an existing licence and the documents to accompany the application. Paragraph 3 requires an applicant for the conversion of an existing licence to give a copy of his application (with its accompanying documents) to the chief officer of police for the police area in which the premises are situated within 48 hours of the application. In circumstances where an appeal is pending against a decision to revoke or reject an application for the renewal of an existing licence and the chief officer of police is satisfied that the conversion of the existing licence would undermine the crime prevention objective or where he is satisfied that there has been a material change in circumstances since the grant of the existing licence or its last renewal such that the conversion of the existing licence would undermine the crime prevention objective, he must give a notice to that effect to both the applicant and the licensing authority. Paragraph 3(5) provides that the chief officer of police may not give such a notice after the end of the period of 28 days beginning with the day on which he received a copy of the application.

315. By virtue of paragraph 4, a licensing authority must grant the application for conversion of an existing licence unless a notice has been given by the chief officer of police under paragraph 3 which has not been withdrawn. If a notice has been given, the authority must hold a hearing to consider that notice (unless the applicant, the chief officer of police and the licensing authority agree that this is unnecessary) and reject the application (or that part of the application which relates to the existing licence to which the notice relates) if the authority considers that it is necessary to do so for the promotion of the crime prevention objective. If the licensing authority fails to determine the application within 2 months of the receipt of the application, the application will be treated as granted. However, an application will not be granted in circumstances where the existing licence has ceased to be held by the applicant before the application is granted. Paragraph 6 provides that where a new premises licence is granted the mandatory conditions for such licences will apply.

316. Paragraph 7 provides that a person who makes an application for the conversion of an existing licence may at the same time apply for a variation of the new premises licence (the converted licence), notwithstanding the fact that at that time it would not have been granted, as if that licence is in force under section 37 (application to vary licence to specify individual as premises supervisor) or section 34 (application to vary premises licence). If such an application is made the relevant licensing authority (see section 12) may discharge its functions in relation to that application and the relevant provisions in Part 3 of the Act will apply.

317. This Part of the Schedule also makes provision for the consequences of an existing licence being revoked by the licensing justices or a court after the grant of the new premises licence but before the second day appointed by the Secretary of State. If this occurs in respect of all the existing licensable activities converted to the new premises licence, the new premises licence will lapse. If it occurs in respect of only some of the said existing licensable activities the licensing authority is obliged to amend the new premises licence to remove those activity or activities from it.

318. Provision is made for the applicant to appeal against a decision by the licensing authority to reject the application for conversion of an existing licence and for the chief officer of police to appeal against a decision to grant the application after consideration of his notice of objection. Further, a right of appeal is provided for the "applicant" against a decision to amend the new licence (as mentioned in the paragraph above).

319. These provisions enable existing licence holders, or applicants with their consent, to enjoy the same authorisation in the new system as they currently enjoy if they wish to do so.

320. Provision is made in relation to false statements for the purposes of obtaining a new licence.

321. Paragraph 11 applies where, rather than using the procedure set out in the earlier paragraphs, a person who currently carries on a licensable activity applies for a new premises licence under Part 3 of the Act. A licensing authority is prohibited from attaching conditions to the premises licence which would have the effect of restricting the opening hours to more limited hours than the current "permitted hours" under Part 3 of the Licensing Authority Act 1964.

322. Part 2 of this Schedule makes similar transitional provisions to those in Part 1 in relation to applications by clubs which are registered for the purposes of Part 2 of the Licensing Act 1964 to convert their existing club certificate under that Part to a club premises certificate.

323. Part 3 of this Schedule sets out the transitional provisions for personal licences. During the transitional period (defined as the period of not less than six months specified by order), a holder of an existing justices' licence (granted under the Licensing Act 1964) authorising the sale of alcohol by retail will be entitled to apply for the grant to him of a personal licence without having to possess the licensing qualification ordinarily required under Part 6 of the Act, provided that certain requirements are met. These are that he produces his current justices' licence, his photograph (in a prescribed form) and a statement (if appropriate) relating to his convictions for relevant offences or foreign offences.

324. The applicant must give a copy of the application for a personal licence to the chief officer of police within 48 hours of making the application. The chief officer of police may give an objection notice if he is satisfied, having regard to the applicant's conviction for any relevant offence or foreign offence, that the exceptional circumstances of the case are such that the grant of the licence would undermine the crime prevention objective. If no objection has been made by the police and the licensing authority is satisfied that the applicant holds a justices' licence the application must be granted. If the authority is not satisfied that the applicant holds a licence it must reject the application. If the police have objected to the grant, the licensing authority must hold a hearing (unless the applicant, police and the authority agree otherwise) to consider the objection. As a result of the consideration of the objection notice the licensing authority must reject the application if it considers it necessary for the promotion of the crime prevention objective to do so or grant the application in any other case. Provisions in Part 6 of the Act relating to the notification of determinations by the licensing authority apply in relation to the authority's decision (see section 122). Rights of appeal are conferred on the applicant and the chief officer of police.

325. If an authority fails to determine an application for a personal licence within 3 months of its receipt, the application will be treated as granted.

326. Part 4 of this Schedule provides that during the transitional period licensing authorities should consult representatives of existing justices' licences and registered clubs in their area in forming their licensing policy.

327. Section 191 (meaning of "alcohol") excludes "denatured alcohol". This is the term which, from the commencement of section 5(1) of the Finance Act 1995 is to be used to refer to what is currently referred to as "methylated spirits". Pending the commencement of that provision, section 191 has effect by virtue of paragraph 30 of this Schedule as if it referred to "methylated spirits".

328. The Schedule also makes provision for savings in relation to some of the provisions which are repealed by the Act. To the extent that the provisions repealed are relied

upon in other statutes (in particular, local enactments relating to London) their effect is preserved.

COMMENCEMENT

329. The provisions of the Act will come into force in accordance with the provisions of one or more commencement orders made by the Secretary of State.

HANSARD REFERENCES

330. The following table sets out the dates and Hansard references for each stage of the Act's passage through Parliament.

Stage	***Date***	***Hansard Ref***
House of Lords – Presentation and First Reading	14th November 2002	Vol 641 (no. 2), Col 25
Second Reading	26th November 2002	Vol 641 (no. 8), Col 640
Committee	12th, 17th, 19th December 2002 and 13th, 16th, 20th January 2003	Vol 642 (no.s 18, 20, 22), Cols 331, 537, 785, Vol 643 (no.s 26, 29 30), Cols 11, 301, 435
Report Stage	24th, 27th February 2003 and 4th March 2003	Vol 645 (no.s 50, 53, 56), Cols 10, 379, 709
Third Reading	11th March 2003	Vol 645 (no. 61), Col 1237
House of Commons - First Reading	12th March 2003	
Second Reading	24th March 2003	Vol 402 (no.69), Col 51
Committee Stage	1st, 2nd, 3rd, 10th, 29th April 2003 and 6th, 8th, 13th, 15th, 20th May 2003	**Sc - D**
Remaining stages	16th June 2003	Vol 407 (no. 109), Col 83
Lords' Consideration of Commons' Amendments	19th June 2003	Vol 649 (no. 112), Col 964
Commons' Consideration of Lords' Amendments	24th June 2003	Vol 407 (no. 115), Col 1004
Lords' Consideration of Commons' Amendments	3rd July 2003	Vol 650 (no.122), Col 1046
Commons' Consideration of Lords' Amendments	8th July 2003	Vol 408 (no. 124), Col 1116
Royal Assent –		10th July 2003 - House of Lords Hansard Vol 651 (127) Col 469
		10th July 2003 - House of Commons Hansard Vol 408 (no.126) Col 1429

Adapted and published by GRANGIS under the OGL Licence 3.0.

GRANGIS - UK PUBLISHING 2022.

www.ingramcontent.com/pod-product-compliance
Lightning Source LLC
LaVergne TN
LVHW060214210926
848481LV00008B/2735
9798885590372